DATE			

APR - - 2023

BAKER & TAYLOR

THE
elevation
APPROACH

THE
elevation
APPROACH

Harness the Power of Work-Life Harmony
to Unlock Your Creativity, Cultivate Joy, and
Reach Your Biggest Goals

TINA WELLS

with Stephanie Smith

RODALE

NEW YORK

RODALE BOOKS is a registered trademark, and the Circle colophon is a
trademark of Penguin Random House LLC.

Library of Congress Cataloging-in-Publication Data has been applied for.

ISBN 978-0-593-58024-0
Ebook ISBN 978-0-593-58025-7
Target Edition ISBN 978-0-593-58171-1

Printed in the United States of America

Book design by Andrea Lau
Jacket design by Maia Gantcheva and Irene Ng

10 9 8 7 6 5 4 3 2 1

First Edition

For Mom and Dad, my two greatest teachers

We cannot lower the mountain,
therefore we must elevate ourselves.

—TODD SKINNER

CONTENTS

Introduction   1

getting started

Chapter 1   The Power of Work-Life Harmony   7
Chapter 2 . What Is the Elevation Approach?   22

PHASE ONE

preparation

Chapter 3   The Art of Getting Ready   37
Chapter 4   Principle #1: Declutter Your Spaces   52
Chapter 5   Principle #2: Get Curious   66
Chapter 6   Principle #3: Know Your Numbers   77

PHASE TWO

inspiration

Chapter 7   Inviting Inspiration   87
Chapter 8   Principle #4: Create Rituals   103
Chapter 9   Principle #5: Build Your Tribe   115
Chapter 10 Principle #6: Make Deposits Before
            Withdrawals   131

PHASE THREE
recreation

Chapter 11 Get Ready to Recreate!   149
Chapter 12 Principle #7: Get Outside of Your Safe Zone   160
Chapter 13 Principle #8: Move   171
Chapter 14 Principle #9: Create Joy   179

PHASE FOUR
transformation

Chapter 15 Entering Transformation   193
Chapter 16 Principle #10: Find a Spiritual Practice   209
Chapter 17 Principle #11: Make Space for Reflection   225
Chapter 18 Principle #12: Let Go of What No Longer
            Serves You   239

Some Final Thoughts   253
Bibliography   257
Acknowledgments   259

INTRODUCTION

Hi, friend! I'm so glad you're here. You've got yourself the ultimate guide to elevating your everyday life.

The definition of *elevating*, according to the authorities of the *Oxford Learner's Dictionary*, is "to lift something up or put something in a higher position" or "to make the level of something increase." If we applied this concept to our lives, it would mean raising or lifting our lives to a higher level.

For most people, the idea of elevating your life involves doing things that are in sync with your personal values and interests and that give you a sense of purpose. Elevation might be about getting that dream job or planning a vacation around the world, with stops at the best restaurants and hotels along the way. It might mean taking your health and fitness to the next level or getting better at an activity you enjoy, like cooking or dancing. For some people, it involves major life achievements and changes, like starting a business, moving to a new town, or leaving a relationship. Other people might simply want to feel more relaxed or happier.

For me, elevating my life means living higher, better—to really live as my best self. And I believe that best self is found when there is harmony between work and life. Sure, I want to dream big and achieve my business goals, but I also want to carve out ample space in my schedule for self-care and quality time with my family. Elevating my life means finding room for joy in my daily busy schedule, even for the small things. Elevation, for me, feels like moving with ease and joy toward my big dreams.

Whatever your idea of an elevated life is, you can make it happen. No matter who you are, where you're from, or what your background is, you have the right to live the biggest, happiest, most joyous life you can imagine. And I'm here to help.

I launched my own company, Buzz Marketing Group (BMG), when I was just sixteen years old. Several years later, I was a young, trailblazing businesswoman with Fortune 500 clients that included Dell, Kroger, and Johnson & Johnson. I served on executive boards, wrote children's books, and advised those Fortune 500 companies and their executives on business and personal development. I purchased a beautiful home in South Jersey. I traveled around the world. I had a Rolodex of names and numbers of the most influential business executives in the world. I did all these things while often being the only woman in the room, the only Black woman in the room, or the youngest and only Black woman in the room.

And yet, at times, there was something wrong.

Already, when I was only twenty-seven years old, I found myself in total burnout after eleven years in business. My work suffered, my personal life was impaired, and my health took a hit—ulcers and hair loss occurred because I was working too much. To keep myself going, I made myself take breaks. I booked more vacations and spa appointments, but these small moments of leisure didn't always lead to relaxation. On the contrary, I launched new projects, like my middle-grade fiction book series *Mackenzie Blue*, while I was on sabbatical and far from home. These new ventures launched me from rest and relaxation into the throes of late nights and deadlines. Then, just when those new and exciting projects gained steam, that same burnout returned.

After several rounds of this exhausting cycle, I knew I had to find a different way to work and live, one that would allow me to rest and recover long enough so that I'd be in peak form to run my business. I focused on creating a method that would help me balance my work, creative projects, and personal times without exhausting myself. I wanted something that helped me align my productivity with my creativity, along with built-in time to reflect and regroup—and perhaps most important, time to go on a vacation without feeling anxious because I wasn't checking my emails while I was swimming.

I found my answer in the Elevation Approach. This is my unique, foolproof method to take action and reach your biggest goals, while finding harmony between work and life along the way. I've used the Elevation Approach to launch business ideas and new ventures, with much success. But I've also used it to think through major decisions in my life. For example, when I wanted to move to Brazil in the middle of the pandemic, I used the Elevation Approach to make that decision. When I wanted to launch a course for entrepreneurs, I used the Elevation Approach. When I decided to sell my home, or undergo an IUI (intrauterine insemination), or take a position on the board of a health start-up, I used—you guessed it. I used the Elevation Approach to assess what I wanted to do, to get motivated to do it, to perform the necessary research and prepare for the task, and to dive right in.

Yes, the Elevation Approach has helped me change my life.

Today, I'm mindful to take on only the projects that bring me joy. Not the ones I think I should be doing or the ones that look good on paper; just the ones I will truly be happy to work on every day. I've finally gone on *real* vacations, whether it was riding a camel in Israel, climbing the sand dunes in Namibia, or simply enjoying countless trips to local farms in my native Lancaster, Pennsylvania. I spend quality time with my friends and I enjoy weekly gatherings with my family. I travel the world with my niece. In short, I've loved and lost, made new friends near and far, and written more than a dozen books, all the while tending to my many responsibilities as a founder and CEO, a doting daughter, an auntie, and a friend and mentor to many others.

Best of all, I figured out how to merge my work life and my personal life without making tough tradeoffs. I feel content, grounded, focused, and at peace. Ease, joy, focus, and purpose are the cornerstones of my day.

Using this plan, I'm living a life that takes me well beyond my wildest dreams. So, in this book you'll also learn to use the Elevation Approach to create work-life harmony for yourself, with the help of the tools, real-world examples, worksheets, and journal prompts I've provided. If you want to make a shift in your career, family, relationships, finances, health, fitness, or any other aspect of your life, the Elevation Approach will help you make that happen. Work-life harmony can be found, no matter how busy, tired, or overworked you think you are. Let me show you how.

And one last thing: I wanted to make it easy for you to complete the exercises in the book. You can visit this link to download all the worksheets referenced in this book: elevationtribe.com /resources. Enjoy!

getting started
_____

CHAPTER 1

The Power of Work-Life Harmony

"Do you ever sleep?"

Whenever someone asks me this question, I tell them the truth: "Yes, I do. At least seven and a half hours per night, nonnegotiable."

I'm usually met with a blank stare. "I just don't see how that's possible. How do you do all the things you do? There's just so much. . . ." These questions usually lead to a conversation about a concept that has become the core of my life: work-life harmony.

Different forms of harmony are around us. For instance, we see it reflected in nature every day. I love the outdoors, and I've been super-fortunate to travel to Africa several times. One of the things that struck me on my first safari in Kenya was that nature was just . . . in sync. I sat for hours one morning watching hundreds of zebras and wildebeests migrate from Kenya to Tanzania. They knew where to go and when to go. Another day I watched two cheetahs eat their lunch while vultures nearby waited patiently for the leftovers. When the cheetahs walked away, the vultures descended on the remainders, and it was as if nature had brought its own clean-up crew! Similarly, I picked up on these unspoken rhythms, rising easily with the first sign of light and growing tired when the sun went down. Seeing how everything in nature moves in continuous, complementary ways made me realize how we humans can experience this harmony in our own lives—but how easy it can be for our lives to fall out of tune with that harmony.

Burnout: Everybody's Doing It!

After burning myself out for the first time, when I was twenty-seven years old, I decided to take my first proper vacation since launching my company eleven years prior. When my friend invited me to join her in Miami, she said my laptop wasn't invited. But I didn't think it was possible to unplug: Did she really expect me to not check my email for seven whole days? When we arrived, I was anxious and scatterbrained. I realized that I didn't even know how to stretch out by the pool and relax.

I once approached work with an all-or-nothing attitude. I would get up early and grind away until the late hours. Sure, I had to sleep, but I kept the other sixteen hours of the day, plus the weekends, available for work. To me, this was just the cost of doing business. You see, I was not just the CEO of my own business but also a well-known teen entrepreneur. The story of how I founded my marketing agency followed me everywhere. By the time I was twenty-five, articles about me had appeared in major women's magazines, including a cover story in *O, The Oprah Magazine*. I am so grateful for every experience I had, and I was so blessed to have built a great company, but it was sometimes overwhelming. I went from teen entrepreneur to college student athlete and writer at the school paper, to running an office in New York City after college. I kept barreling ahead.

To be an entrepreneur, you are expected to dedicate yourself to your work, especially when hustle culture was the paradigm for success in American business and "girlbosses" were glorifying the grind. And for a Black woman in business, the self-applied pressure to be twice as good as my counterparts propelled me to work even harder. I was one of the few Black entrepreneurs in marketing at this time. I knew the spotlight was on me, and so I wanted not only to represent my family and my community but also to make them proud.

When things got really busy at Buzz Marketing Group, I just kept going. Instead of delegating the work when different clients launched big projects at the same time, I made myself even more accessible and I dug in deeper. However, that extra dedication came at a cost. I skipped taking vacations because I needed to go on back-to-back work trips. I neglected doctor's appointments and gave up my beloved daily walks. There just was no time for any of that.

Burnout is a familiar experience, particularly now and especially among young women. We've been socialized to give all of ourselves to others and to stretch ourselves to satisfy everyone else's needs before our own. At home, we're constantly serving our families to make sure they're cared for. For those of us who work outside the home, we're likely to volunteer for extra tasks, even when our plates are already full. If a deadline must be met, chances are a woman on the team has volunteered to work those extra hours to ensure that the deadline gets met.

Traditionally, our culture has celebrated working hard for the money (cue that catchy tune by Donna Summer!). For decades, women have fought to gain an equal footing in the workplace, and now that we've come close to achieving that, it's understandable that those who've made it will work hard to keep it (and help bring their fellow ladies along). Nevertheless—and this is true for everyone—our relationship with work slowly becomes an obsession. Corporations offer every amenity employees would want— sleeping pods, healthy (and free) organic snacks, wellness coaches, and office gyms—so that people never have to leave the office. We've all prioritized productivity over well-being. We speak honorably of those who never take vacations or call in sick. We herald young workers who give twelve hours a day to their jobs and create side hustles on social media.

While success seems to be within easy reach for those who give blood, sweat, and tears to an organization, this attitude usually leaves us exhausted, anxious, and stressed. In 2020, a Gallup poll of more than 12,000 workers found that about 76 percent of workers reported experiencing some sort of burnout on the job. The World Health Organization (WHO) has recognized burnout as an occupational phenomenon, defined as "a syndrome . . . resulting from chronic workplace stress that has not been successfully managed."

While the WHO pinpoints workplace stress as the source of burnout, that burnout also happens when there is too much to do at home. More women than ever are the breadwinners or heads of their households. And historically, women are usually the caregivers for loved ones, such as a child or an aging parent. In the United States, the typical caregiver for an elderly family member is a forty-nine-year-old woman who provides twenty hours a week of unpaid care. Also, women spend twice as much time per day taking care of children than men.

Couple these household responsibilities with an already burdensome work life and a seemingly unending pandemic, and you get an inevitable burnout at home, too. To make matters worse, the emotional exhaustion from caregiving burnout makes it a whole different beast from work-related burnout—something I discovered firsthand when I became the primary caregiver for my dad after one of his surgeries.

When Covid-19 hit in 2020, the situation reached a tipping point. People were forced to work from home, blurring the lines between workspace and personal space. In essence, employees invited their managers into their living rooms when they took Zoom calls. Working hours got extended well past the nine-to-five schedule. If you were a parent, though, you also needed to tutor your children while they navigated online schooling. And you had to secure your home, or at least your elderly relatives, from exposure to the virus.

During this time, we started to reevaluate the relationship between work and success, examining how our work lives and our personal lives were intertwined. We wondered whether commuting, much less spending hours in an office, was worth our time. We questioned whether the work we were doing felt fulfilling. We asked ourselves hard questions about how we worked, what we did for work, and why we did the work we did. And a time when the future of the world was unclear, when our health became a top priority as we navigated the pandemic, we wondered if we were prioritizing our own lives as much as we did our jobs.

The pandemic was a catalyst. It inspired us to seek a better way of allocating our time and energy. Now, people don't just want jobs with good pay and great perks; they also want jobs that allow them to enjoy their lives, both at work and away from it. No longer are we living to work or working to live. The new standard for work in a postpandemic world is a life that prioritizes both our well-being and our personal fulfillment—that takes a holistic approach to how we satisfy our needs.

Out with Work-Life Balance . . .

Back in the day, I thought my work-life balance allowed me to pack my days with as much as I could. All I needed to do was separate my work from my life. If I could create separate, color-coded windows for my relationship, my family, my friends, and my work, and cut out unnecessary tasks, I could make time for anything I wanted to do.

What happened instead was that I was always working, even when I was supposed to be off. Family photos featured me on my phone or consumed with something happening on-screen. I said yes to new obligations without a second thought. When my dad started getting sick, I volunteered to help my mom take care of him—that, on top of all my work responsibilities. When I had a meltdown in front of my sisters, they asked me, "Why did you think you had to do this all on your own?" I couldn't answer their question. It never occurred to me that I didn't have to do it all by myself.

Having a work-life balance may sound like the solution for doing everything that matters most to you, but it's an antiquated way to think about how we should live our lives today. Here's why we need to move on from this ineffective framework:

- **WORK-LIFE BALANCE FORCES AN EITHER/OR APPROACH TO WORK AND LIFE:** The idea of work-life balance assumes your work life and personal life are separate. It doesn't account for the possibility that your work life will encroach upon your personal life or that your personal life will affect your performance at the office. We simply don't live in these silos anymore, particularly as our work habits and home lives have changed. We now set up offices in our bedrooms and we schedule meetings around—or in some cases, during—school pickup times and dinner.

- **WORK-LIFE BALANCE DOESN'T CONSIDER YOUR EMOTIONS ABOUT WORK OR ITS EMOTIONAL EFFECTS ON YOUR LIFE:** Work-life balance assumes that life is ideal when time spent at work and time spent outside of work are equal. But attaining that ideal does not always bring happiness or allow us to consider how we want our days to feel. For example, many working parents may spend a dedicated amount of time at work, but they still feel guilt at work when they are away from their children. Conversely, they may feel guilt at home for leaving the office to attend a school function.

  The work-life balance may mean nothing if you're miserable at your job and at home, and you don't have any tools to bring joyful moments to your days. Or, it may be that your work is so emotionally taxing that the resulting burnout, frustration, or depression carries over into your personal life, no matter how early you leave on Fridays.

  Workers also shouldn't have to abandon their work to enjoy their lives, nor should joy be solely reserved for their time outside the office. Some people are happy working intently at work for eleven or twelve hours a day because they truly love what they do. For others, work may serve as a helpful distraction from or coping mechanism for dealing with personal matters.

- **WORK-LIFE BALANCE DOESN'T CONSIDER OTHER PARTS OF YOUR LIFE THAT NEED TENDING:** Though the "life" part of work-life balance refers to the things you do away from your desk, there are aspects of your everyday routines, such as your physical health (including your sleep and nutritional habits), your mental health, or your relationships, that don't fall neatly into either of those categories. Additionally, a framework that places the work-life balance on a pedestal doesn't account for unforeseen situations, where equal attention to both parts of your life just aren't possible. For example, your health might need more attention if you fall ill or become injured. Or, maybe caring for a sick relative for an extended time requires you to take your focus off work. Sometimes, throwing your life off-balance is exactly what you need to do.

- **WORK-LIFE BALANCE DOESN'T PREVENT YOU FROM TAKING ON TOO MANY RESPONSIBILITIES:** Balance implies an equal distribution between two things—in this case, work and life. In theory, if you add more work, you must add more life to maintain the balance. If you want to start a side hustle and maintain your work-life balance, you need to devote more attention to your personal life to "make up for" the time spent on your new work endeavor. But that's twice as much activity as you were looking to do. You could take on 100 different jobs and 100 different life responsibilities, dedicate yourself equally to them all, and still technically have a work-life balance. But would this make you happy? Where does the burden end? How heavy a load should you carry? Chasing work-life balance doesn't give you the answers to these questions.

. . . In with Work-Life Harmony

Since I've sought work-life harmony, I approach my days completely differently. My schedule includes more unscheduled blocks of time for things that make me smile.

I spend time in the morning preparing for the day—reading, listening to podcasts, or cooking. Afterward, I have meetings and take calls, becoming more visible and social. In midafternoon, it's time for a break. I try to find time for a walk or a moment to sit outside for fifteen minutes, feel the sunshine, and breathe in clean air. Then, I tackle the more reflective or analytical tasks in the later afternoon. There are times when I continue reading and working until I go to bed. But these moments never feel forced. They are completely my choice.

But harmony is more than how you schedule your work tasks. In music, harmony happens when two or more contrasting melodies are played together. In your everyday life, harmony happens when you integrate your personal life and work life so your day flows smoothly. My days feel more fluid and are so full of activities that they serve both my personal and professional needs. That is, the parts of my life complement one another, rather than working in opposition.

Here's why this alternative to work-life balance elevates your life:

- **WORK-LIFE HARMONY PUTS YOU FIRST, NOT WORK FIRST:** You are the nexus around which your life revolves. Work-life harmony helps you evaluate whether the things in your life are in sync with your priorities. That means you determine how much work, play, and everything in between you need and want.

- **WORK-LIFE HARMONY HELPS YOU ALIGN YOUR LIFE'S PUR-POSE WITH YOUR WORK AND PERSONAL PURSUITS:** Rather than shifting gears, overhauling your schedule, and doubling down on your efforts because one aspect of your day-to-day feels imbalanced, work-life harmony gives you a bird's-eye view of your entire life. Because you can see how your everyday activities, your environment, your health, and the things you consume affect you, it becomes easier to choose the activities that enhance your life and eliminate those that don't.

- **WORK-LIFE HARMONY ALLOWS YOU TO CHOOSE YOUR PRI-ORITIES AND MOVE IN SYNC WITH THEM:** The work-life harmony helps you find a way to navigate the different parts of your life. For example, if you need to take a call and pick the kids up from camp, why choose one or the other? With work-life harmony, you can do both in a way that won't leave you feeling exhausted. You might prefer to take that call while you're in the car on the way to pick up your kids. Need to review a document for the next day? Do you prefer to wait until after the kids go to bed? Work-life balance says you should choose to do your work at work, and your home activities when you're at home. Work-life harmony says you should choose to work when you want to or do home activities when you want to, in a way that fits your schedule and preferences.

- **WORK-LIFE HARMONY HELPS YOU PRIORITIZE TASKS BASED ON PERSONAL FULFILLMENT AND SATISFACTION:** Work-life harmony allows you to decide how you want to feel when you do the things you do and when you choose your activities based on whether they will produce those feelings. For example, choosing to work a job you don't enjoy so you can afford weekend vacations to the beach may be an example of work-life balance, but are you truly content with this arrangement? Instead, leaning into work-life harmony would involve your finding a way to feel as peaceful as you do at the beach during both your working hours and your free time. That might mean changing your work habits or even finding a new job that's related to your interest in oceans or located in a beach town.

- **WORK-LIFE HARMONY ALLOWS YOU TO NAVIGATE THE CHALLENGES THAT LIFE THROWS YOUR WAY:** Work-life balance implies choosing either work or life at one time to focus your time on, so an unexpected event (whether positive or negative) can feel destabilizing. Work-life harmony allows for those times when you need more focus on work or your personal life, depending on deadlines or emergencies that come up. You don't need to feel like your life is thrown off the rails; you have tools to help you recalibrate your routines and habits as needed.

Find Your Work-Life Harmony

I am sure you're already wondering, *How am I going to apply the ideas in this book and do all of the thousands of things on my to-do list?* I promise you, you'll find a solution. (And while I am not sure you'll get to do everything on your to-do list, you will *feel* as if you did!)

So, how did I find my way to work-life harmony? There were a handful of guiding actions that led me there.

1. I PAID ATTENTION TO MY BODY AND ITS REACTIONS: When I started looking for work-life harmony, I read *Do Less* by my friend Kate Northup (see page 220). The book is a guide for helping women work smarter, not harder, by leaning into the things that matter most. Her idea of body first, business second was a game changer.

I had been trying to make more time for myself by life-hacking my way through my to-do list, but I wasn't getting more done. When I realized I should focus on my body and what I needed, I started watching my reactions to certain situations. I discovered I was doing things that didn't make me feel good. I overcommitted myself to other people's causes and I kept taking on more and more family responsibilities. I was anxious, irritated, hypersensitive, and restless. Additionally, I was missing a spiritual practice, which is usually something I tuned into to help ground me. All the data points for my physical health (such as my weight and A1C levels) were off. For example, if I felt myself physically contracting or getting anxious on my way to an event that I didn't even have to attend, then that was something I had to remove from my life.

The next time you're starting to feel this way, do a check on your body. Are you feeling tense? In which areas? Are you breathing deeply and in a relaxed way, or is your breathing shallow and rushed? Are you feeling hopeful and happy right now? Or are you anxious and nervous, like something bad is about to happen?

2. I PUT MY PASSIONS FIRST: After paying attention to my body's reactions, I started asking myself: "What do I really love? What do I personally want to do?" I realized I am passionate about creating things. I love the process of making something out of nothing and working with a team to bring a vision to reality. Whether it's a book like the one you're reading now or a fun gift basket for friends, I knew I needed to create.

3. I LOOKED BEYOND WORK TO DO WHAT I LOVE: If my passion was creating things, it didn't need to be something I did only at work. In fact, my work didn't leave me with many opportunities to do what I truly loved. I had spent decades managing creatives at BMG, not creating anything myself! No wonder I burned out!

I realized that I'd find work-life harmony if I focused on filling my life with the things and people I love. I love art and design, home renovations, and above all, a good party! I love creating themes and invites, as well as everything else that goes into holding a great event. I also love spending time with people who enjoy those same things. For instance, my niece, Phoebe, loves to cook. From the time she was little, she'd come into my kitchen and make a total mess with her "experiments." We'd spend so much time mixing up all kinds of things. She's older now, and we still love cooking together.

To figure out what passions you should prioritize, notice which activities boost your mood. What do you like reading or learning about when you have free time? What are you passionate about?

4. I STARTED WITH SMALL MOMENTS: Though I was an entrepreneur who managed her own calendar, I often felt I had no control over my day. When I moved toward work-life harmony instead of work-life balance, I began having more say about what I was doing with my day. I started by finding pockets of time when I could begin to experience that harmony. While I got ready each morning, I listened to a personally curated news briefing. Even if I were on the phone, in a meeting, or on Zoom all day, those first thirty minutes were just for me.

Let's say you're working eight to ten hours per day and those hours are dictated by your boss. How can you move toward harmony? Can you turn your commute into a time when you experience harmony? Can you listen to some blissful music before you hop along to your next Zoom call? Can you step away from what you're doing for five minutes just to walk around in some fresh air?

5. I DID LESS TO MAKE MORE TIME FOR MYSELF: To set aside time for myself, I implemented a "doing less" system whereby I didn't take meetings on Mondays and Fridays. Because no one really wants to hear that you're unavailable (and you might not be able to say no to your boss), I presented this change as a personal preference. I told clients, "I prefer to have my Mondays and Fridays be strategy days, when I do the big thinking around how to best serve you." This was well received because they appreciated how thoughtfully I arranged my schedule and were happy to accommodate my request.

You can set up a similar system. For instance, if you need a little alone time before you get your family ready for the day, you could tell your loved ones, "You know what? If you can give me twenty minutes in the morning, I am going to be so much more ready to spend the day with you." Let people know they'll get your very best self when you have a moment to be by yourself.

6. I REMEMBERED I WAS WORTH THE EFFORT: As I was trying to create my work-life harmony, I had to keep reminding myself that I had to change for my health, to create wealth, and to elevate my life. I also had to remind myself that I was worth it. So often as Black women we are made to feel we're just not as valuable, or as valued, as others. As women—and honestly, as people—we are used to other people giving us our value. I will be honest with you: getting to the work-life harmony I have now was a process, and it was *my* process. I did not need anyone's permission to seek this harmony for myself, and you don't, either. Not your partner, not your family, not your boss.

Once I decided to move toward the work-life harmony I wanted, things started to fall into place. I was spending my days creating things I was truly passionate about, with people I really enjoyed, and I was making time and space for rituals and other things that mattered to me. Once I prioritized *myself*, I was also a much better person to be around. My sisters started commenting on how much fun I had become. Random strangers commented on my glow. Friends texted me that I looked so happy. And I wasn't just happy— I'd found joy.

My greatest hope for you is that you drop the weight that accompanies work-life balance and embrace the freedom and lightness of work-life harmony. I think back to my first trip to Africa, when I watched in awe as nature did her thing. Now I watch my life flow in the same way.

CHAPTER 2

What Is the Elevation Approach?

There's a saying that goes "A goal without a plan is just a wish." Think about the things you have wanted, or still want, in your life, especially the ambitions and hopes that motivated you to buy this book. Now, think about why those goals haven't come to fruition yet. You might have had a vision of who you want to be or how you want to feel, but you don't know how to get there. You might have been pursuing a big, bold, life-altering dream, but you suddenly got stuck. Maybe you haven't gotten started working toward realizing your dream because life keeps throwing challenges your way. You can't imagine squeezing another activity into your day when you already have so much to do.

Setting a goal and achieving it have always been easier said than done, but they're especially hard if you don't have a road map to get you where you want to go. A road map is exactly what the Elevation Approach provides. It is designed to move you from wishing you could do something to making that wish come true.

The Elevation Approach is my method for working toward

any goal, no matter how mundane or complex. It offers a cycle of activities that help you make a plan, take action, create accountability, and think through challenges. Whenever I've needed to launch a new business idea, navigate a major life decision, or make an important change in my routine, the Elevation Approach has been my North Star. It has helped me designate time for the tasks that will make my life better, figure out the steps I need to take for achieving my goals, and help me maintain my momentum and/or pace myself during busy times. More important, the Elevation Approach provides the tools I can use to create work-life harmony and build into my routine the practices described on pages 17–20.

Our dreams don't have expiration dates. No matter where you are in life, or what your life looks like right now, the Elevation Approach will help you find a place where deep joy meets a sense of purpose.

Elevate Your Goal Setting

Achieving work-life harmony involves creating systems that allow the different parts of your life to work together, not against one another. You might think this means you need to revamp your life and start again from scratch. I don't blame you! We're often asked to buy into a new tool, gadget, or program that comes with a grandiose promise to improve our lives, whether it's to cook better, look younger, or live longer.

Though it might be tempting to start from scratch, working from a clean slate might be counterproductive, especially if you already have activities that make your life meaningful and routines that help it run smoothly. The Elevation Approach won't ask you to abandon those parts of your life that are working—and it certainly won't ask you to abandon your present life just to get started. Instead, we begin with a task that might already be familiar: setting a goal.

Work-life harmony starts by making sure your goals are aligned with the feelings and environment you want to cultivate in your life. Many of us are used to setting goals because we want to meet our own expectations or those of our loved ones and peers. Some of us may also set certain goals to produce a desired effect—like establishing a sense of stability, safety, or confidence—at the expense of devoting energy to those projects that mean the most to us. Here, you'll learn how to define a goal that puts your interests, passions, and dreams first.

How to Make "Elevated" Goals

The goal you set with the Elevation Approach can be as big or as small as you like. It can be a onetime event, such as planning a big party for your best friend's fortieth birthday, or it can be setting a life-changing milestone, such as adopting a child. Your goal might be to carve out more space in your life for an activity. For example, perhaps you'd like to find an hour every morning to meditate and practice yoga; maybe you'd like to take a mural-painting class or spend more time with your elderly family members.

With so many possibilities to choose from, how do you know which goals will work best for you? Here are some guidelines to keep in mind:

- **YOUR GOAL SHOULD HELP YOU LIVE A MORE JOYOUS LIFE:** The Elevation Approach works best if you choose a goal you're passionate about. This goal should be something that will bring you joy as you complete it. For example, if you love spending time outside, maybe start with a small goal of making weekly trips to the local park. Or, you could take on a longer-term project, like building a backyard garden or starting a hiking club for nature lovers in your area.

- **YOUR GOAL SHOULD ADDRESS SOMETHING THAT IS MISSING FROM YOUR LIFE:** Assess where you are in your life and what parts of it you'd like to change or improve. If you're trying to find more time for play, choosing a career-focused goal won't necessarily help you accomplish that goal.

- **YOUR GOAL SHOULD ALIGN WITH YOUR VALUES:** You should be aware of what your life values are and how your goal would fit with them. For example, do you value spending time with your family? Then it might make sense to plan a siblings-only camping trip or host monthly family game nights. If you live far from your family, your goal might be to organize a reunion or perhaps plan a cross-country move so you can be closer to your loved ones.

- **START WITH A SMALL GOAL:** Set yourself up for success with an attainable goal to which you can dedicate ample time. We should always dream big, but we should also give ourselves time to thrive. If you want to become a runner, you don't start by trying to run a marathon; maybe train for a 5K race and then build up to a 10K. Give yourself a sensible starting point and the time to gather your resources, plan your approach, and work toward meeting that small goal; ultimately, this will help you accomplish bigger goals as well.

- **CHOOSE A GOAL YOU WANT:** Choose a goal you actually want for yourself. Don't feel the pressure to choose something you "should" be doing. We're used to feeling like we need to meet society's outmoded standards—you should be married by age thirty, you should own a home, you should have two kids and a dog. None of those goals are necessary if you don't want them.

- **CHOOSE A GOAL THAT DOESN'T FEEL LIKE WORK:** The goal you set for yourself should be something you're excited to tackle; it shouldn't seem like a mundane task on a daily to-do list or a never-ending slog.

Exercise: Moving Closer to Yes

It's easy to get excited about a new dream without checking whether it will bring you work-life harmony. I use this exercise in the early phases of setting a goal. Complete this quick questionnaire by putting down on paper some thoughts about your goal; it will help you hone in on why it can make your life better.

Answer these three questions:

1. Why did I choose this goal?
2. What do I hope to accomplish in one month, six months, one year, or three to five years? (Use the amount of time of your choice.)
3. How will my life be different when I accomplish this goal?

Asking yourself these deceptively simple questions will help you think deeply about why you want to accomplish something. It will also set you up to believe that your goal is something worth pursuing!

Exercise: Get "SMART" About Goal Setting

The Elevation Approach is more effective if you can clearly define your goal. A popular way to outline the details of a goal is to use the SMART goal framework. SMART is an acronym, meaning Specific, Measurable, Achievable, Relevant, and Time-based. Outlining a goal using these elements will allow you to map out what your goal is, what you need to achieve it, and how much time it will take you to get you there.

For example, let's assume your goal is to renovate your basement. Using the SMART framework, it might look something like this:

SPECIFIC: I want to renovate my basement and turn it into a game room.

MEASURABLE: I will add four new features to the space: a pool table, a Ping-Pong table, a new television, and a bar.

ACHIEVABLE: I will buy the pool table at the billiards store, the Ping-Pong table and television online, and hire a contractor to build the bar. The total cost will be $10,000 and that is within my budget.

RELEVANT: The new game room will allow our family to spend more time together and to host fun events for our friends.

TIME-BASED: I can get the renovation done in the next six months.

You can use the worksheet on page 28 to help you define your goal. Incorporate the details that you fill in the boxes next to each letter of SMART into the description of your goal.

S

M

A

R

T

GOAL

COMPLETED BY

How the Elevation Approach Works

I've described the Elevation Approach as a cycle of activities that help you to make a plan, take action, create accountability, and think through challenges. What do I mean by a cycle? How long will it take to achieve that work-life harmony I speak so highly of? Is this effort going to be a year's worth of work before you see results? Now that you've picked a goal to use with the Elevation Approach, let's learn how the cycle works.

The Four Phases

The Elevation Approach consists of four phases. Similar to the phases of the moon, these phases are set up to run one right after another.

Each of the four phases will help you reach your goal:

- **PREPARATION**: This is the time for planning. You gather the materials, tools, and resources you need to get started and you evaluate what you can realistically provide for your new project.
- **INSPIRATION**: This is when you seek out the books, images, places, and people that spark your creative energy. You kick-start your new idea and open yourself up to the world around you.
- **RECREATION**: This is when you take a break from your work. You indulge in a bit of fun to recharge your batteries, try activities unrelated to your goal, and allow yourself to take a breather.
- **TRANSFORMATION**: This is the phase for action and then reflection. You dive into the work you need to do to achieve

your goal. Then, you assess the results, considering how the work has made you feel and the progress you've attained.

Within each of these four phases are three principles that offer a quick boost to your everyday routine. These principles teach you the skills you need and include simple exercises that will help you complete the phase and give your life an instant upgrade. You know that feeling of using your best dinnerware to elevate a dinner gathering? Taking the long way home and smelling the flowers? That's the feeling these principles will provide.

The twelve principles also include advice from the people in my life who have taught me lessons and strategies that have helped me find work-life harmony. These "Instant Elevation" sidebars share personal experiences and words of wisdom from my friends, mentors, business leaders, and even my own mother and show you how they've applied the principles of the Elevation Approach to their own lives.

The tasks in each principle will also help you create practices, build systems, and strengthen the muscles you need to create work-life harmony. Not only will these newly acquired habits and small shifts in thinking bring you individual moments of joy but they will train you to check that your day-to-day efforts are in sync with your other priorities, projects, and responsibilities.

By using the Elevation Approach to work toward your goals, you'll incrementally create your work-life harmony. That is, each moment of uplift and each opportunity will take you a small step toward your goal. With practice, you'll learn how to keep and build the systems that keep the different facets of your life working together, even if you're dedicating a large amount of time to meeting your goal. You will even become so attuned to this rhythm that you'll immediately notice if something is off.

Your Life, Your Elevation Approach

The Elevation Approach is designed to be flexible to your needs and to work within your goals, no matter what they are. Since work-life harmony can mean different things to different people, there are no set-in-stone parameters for how your process should progress. For example:

- **YOU CAN START WITH ANY PHASE YOU LIKE:** The first phase of the Elevation Approach is Preparation, but that doesn't mean you can't dive into one of the other phases whenever you want. If you're returning to a goal you've tried pursuing before, for instance, you might want to skip to Transformation, so that you can evaluate your past efforts. If you're crushing it at work and find yourself too burnt out to get started on meeting a personal goal, you might start with Recreation. Don't be afraid to adapt the phases to your needs, jumping to the phase most helpful for your current situation. And if you're unsure about where to begin, you'll find a set of questions at the end of each phase. You can ask those questions to determine if you're ready to jump to the next phase. In fact, use these questions as a guide for deciding where to begin, if needed.
- **TAKE THE TIME YOU NEED:** The timeline for using the Elevation Approach depends on your goal or task. For big, long-term goals, you might need to spend a few weeks or even months in each phase. For smaller goals, a few hours may be enough. Also, there might be situations when you need more time in one particular phase. For example, if you're contemplating a second career after having taken some time off from work, you might spend more time in the

Preparation phase, taking classes, drafting a new résumé, or researching potential clients, and need less time in the Recreation phase. This book gives you the tools for assessing whether you're ready for a new phase or helping to keep you moving if you feel stuck.

- **YOU CAN DIVE INTO AND OUT OF PHASES OR PRINCIPLES AS YOU NEED:** You can dip into and out of the principles for each phase and corresponding activities at will to offer instant moments of uplift. You also may start by integrating a few key principles from another phase into your day, even though they might be unrelated to your goal or your current phase. You may find that the more familiar you become with the Elevation Approach, the easier or more necessary doing some phases becomes. Use this flexibility to adapt the Elevation Approach to your needs.

The Cycles of the Elevation Approach

Transformation may be the fourth phase in the Elevation Approach cycle, but that phase is not the end of your journey. It's not about declaring victory. It's not just a destination arrived at. Coming to the end of the four phases and their corresponding principles doesn't mean you're done; it simply means you've reached the end of one cycle. You can kick-start a new cycle and begin the Elevation Approach again.

That is, achieving harmony in your life requires repeated reevaluation and realignment, as new opportunities or challenges appear in your life. Thus, the Elevation Approach can be used repeatedly to guide you in these redirections, ultimately moving toward work-life harmony. You can repeat the cycle as many times as you feel necessary, so long as you're looking to create harmony in your life.

You can, of course, also start a new cycle if you want to pursue a different goal. Suppose you're working on meeting a continuous, long-term goal; if you find yourself with an unexpected outcome at the end of the Transformation phase, a restart at the beginning of the Elevation Approach can be helpful. That's because restarting with the Preparation phase allows you to assess if you still have the tools you need and if you're still on the right path. During the Inspiration phase, you might take some time to look outside your own work and seek fresh ideas, ones you didn't consider in the previous cycle. Or, after taking a little mental break in the Recreation phase to catch your breath, you can reflect and assess if anything has changed when you begin the Transformation phase. In short, it's lather, rinse, and repeat as needed.

Ready to Dive In?

Take a deep breath and give all this a moment to settle in. As you go forth on this journey, remember to grant yourself some space and grace to discover new things and learn new processes. Change is tricky, but it's also a catalyst for growth.

You might be wondering, *How do I know if I'm doing this right?* You'll know if you feel that things are just getting easier. Do the more challenging tasks now feel less challenging? Does your decision-making process go smoother now? Do you feel you're more focused and more in the present? That's the Elevation Approach at work. This means of thinking through life's big questions and desires will help you feel more at ease. Remember, this method puts work-life harmony first.

And when you've found that harmony in your life, you'll discover that success isn't just something you attain; it's a state of being in which you live every day. Work, play, and everything in between should be enjoyed as much as possible.

So, use the phases and principles of the Elevation Approach to get what you need from your life and to guide you in meeting any new challenges or ventures that pop up. Then, you'll gain the confidence in your ability that will make big things happen. Remember: enjoy time to pursue things that make your soul sing. With the Elevation Approach, you can create a well-rounded life that feels oh so fulfilling and joyous. Now, let's tackle that goal and put the Elevation Approach into motion!

PHASE ONE

PREPARATION

INSPIRATION

TRANSFORMATION

RECREATION

preparation

CHAPTER 3

The Art of Getting Ready

If there's one thing most people readily associate with success, it's preparation. For some goals, preparation might feel intuitive. For instance, many people understand that to cook food, you need ingredients. To take a test, you need to study. Want to paint a picture? You need paints, a canvas or paper, and an idea of what you want to create. But for other goals, your first move might not be as straightforward or simple.

My health has always been one of my top priorities. I've made sure to eat foods that are good for me and I exercise regularly, both to maintain a healthy weight and to manage some hereditary blood sugar issues. But in the last few years, two major things happened: I turned forty years old, and the Covid pandemic upended my life. Though the pandemic certainly made keeping up with my healthy habits a bit more challenging, I tried to stick with my routines. I aimed to exercise three or four days a week and to follow a relatively healthy diet, as before.

At the end of 2020, I went to the doctor for a checkup. He did a comprehensive physical assessment, measuring levels of my hormones, cholesterol, A1C, and more. Boy, did I get a wakeup call! My readings were way out of whack. But when I saw where things were headed, I knew I had to make changes to my diet and my lifestyle.

I was facing this problem not because I didn't already have healthy habits but because the food choices and workout routines I'd followed for decades were no longer working. Now that I was in my forties, my body had changed—and my body's response to diet and exercise changed, too. As such, I needed to adapt my old habits to my body's new composition to get my health back to where it should be. My goal was to reverse the immediate damage and to maintain the positive results of my health makeover.

I used the Elevation Approach to help me make the changes. I tracked my weight and the number of hours I was sleeping. I cleaned up my diet, adding intermittent fasting to my routine to better control my blood sugar issues. I also researched new superfoods and supplements. I increased the number of steps I took each day and even signed up for a few virtual fitness classes to change up my workouts. Several months later, my levels had improved. I lost 15 pounds, and my clothes fit better. I eat more whole foods and vegetables than ever before. I wake up with more energy and more stamina to do the things I want to do.

When I started, I wasn't sure where to begin. If my familiar routines weren't working anymore, what was I supposed to do now? What changes would have the most impact? How would I know if my first move was the right one?

It was the Preparation phase that helped me move forward. Without that phase, it would have been much easier to stay in la-la land and much harder to know which actions were needed to get healthy. Working through the Preparation phase helped me equip myself with the necessary tools and information and enabled me to decide which diet and exercise improvements would best serve my body. The work I did in this phase also provided the clarity and confidence I needed to proceed. That is, I knew the steps I was taking to improve my health would be the right ones because they were informed by research, hard numbers, and deep thinking,

Welcoming something new—and better—into your life requires figuring out what your path to change will look like. Here's how the Preparation phase can help you find your starting point and encourage your first steps forward.

Preparation in Many Forms

Preparation is the phase in which you begin creating your action plan for reaching your goal. Your prep work will take several different forms, including mental, physical, people, data, financial, and schedule preps. For instance, you will need to outline exactly what you need to get going, from the gear you need to the people you can turn to for help. And you will need to prepare your spaces—both the physical and the mental—to make room for those materials you'll gather and the new ideas that will come. Also, you'll prepare your spirit, taking stock of where you are so you can see where you want to be.

If all this is making your head spin, here's how you can break your planning into approachable tasks and then start asking the right questions.

Mental Preparation

Before you turn your attention to anything specific, you need to prepare your mind. Remember, where the mind goes, the body will follow. You need to *believe* it's possible to achieve your goal and you need to *trust* that the work you'll do is meaningful. Without changing your belief systems about yourself and your abilities, it will be impossible to make lasting progress.

When I wanted to make lifestyle changes for my health, I had to shift my thinking. Before, I had believed I'd always done the right things: *I worked out. I ate right. I lost weight before.* Now, I had to acknowledge that my body had changed: *It has different needs now. It's possible I need to upgrade my health routines. I am capable of changing my habits.* Mental preparation is a bit like this: You are preparing to welcome a child into your home. You would need to evaluate your beliefs about what it means to be a good parent. You might think about the values you want to model, decide how you'll handle misbehaviors, and examine where your ideas about parenting come from.

Mental preparation also requires you get brutally honest with yourself and take a cold, hard look at your current situation. You might have heard this before, but I'm saying it now because we all have ways of ignoring inconvenient truths or assuming our discontent is temporary. You need to be willing to give yourself the reality check you need, especially when something in your life is just not working. For instance, if your goal is to end a relationship, you need to ready yourself to have a tough conversation with your partner and be clear about the reasons why you want to break up.

Mental preparation may include answering questions like these:

- What becomes possible if you work toward this goal?
- What are your doubts, worries, or fears about completing this goal or project?

- How long have you wanted to make this change in your life? What have you been ignoring?
- How will you feel if you don't do anything to make this change happen?
- How will you feel if you do reach your goal?

Exercise: Craft Your Vision Statement

When I give business advice to aspiring entrepreneurs, I recommend they create a vision statement. A vision statement functions as your personal contract for making your goal happen; it defines your vision for yourself and for your life. It helps you explain the reasons behind why you do what you do.

For example, when I thought about my vision for my health, I saw myself being healthy enough to pursue every possibility I wanted in life, including being a parent. Having the ability to fully participate in my life because of my health was important to me, so in my vision statement, I wrote this:

I, Tina Wells, am a healthy person. I eat healthy foods packed with vitamins to fuel my body and feed my mind. I exercise regularly and will always research ways to keep my body in optimal health. I stay healthy in order to run my business with a strong mind and body, to ready my body to have a baby if I so choose, and to have the stamina to travel the world.

Now it's your turn. Write down your personal vision statement for a big goal. Explain what your personal vision for your life is and how your goal fits into this vision. Explain why your goal is something you want. Be specific, but think big!

Physical Preparation

Physical preparation is the most tactical type of preparation. You assess what materials, ingredients, or tools you need to procure, as well as take steps to clean out a desk, room, or area to work on your goal. After my doctor's visit, my physical preparations led me to buy an Oura Ring to track my sleep and a new scale to monitor my weight. I also updated my Apple Watch with a bunch of fitness tracking apps. To continue the earlier analogy, if you're planning to become a new parent, you need to set up the child's room and purchase diapers, clothes, toys, and more supplies. Or, if you're unhappy in your relationship, you might need to pack up your belongings in your shared home and move them to your own place.

As you're sourcing your supplies, consider these questions:

- Do you have a space where you can work? What do you need to make this space feel inviting and productive?
- Do you have the tools you need to do what you need to do? If you're beginning a new sport, do you have the equipment or gear you need?
- Do you have the books or reference materials you may need?
- Is there any physical preparation you need to do to take on this goal?

People Preparation

Consider the people you might want to surround yourself with as you move forward with your goal. These people can include close friends and family, colleagues, professionals, and even casual acquaintances. Anyone who can help you reach your goal can be a resource. If you're looking to improve your health, would you seek out a nutritionist or trainer to help you? What about your friend who has run a few marathons and goes to a regular Pilates class? If you're an expecting parent, do you have your doctors in place to care for you and your child? Will you have a babysitter or nanny to help you? If ending your relationship is on your mind, is there anyone you can talk to about your latest fight?

I dive into a discussion of personal relationships in phase two, Inspiration, but here are some quick questions to answer about the people in your life:

- Do you know people who have done something similar to your goal? Are there peers you can call for information and support?
- Are there experts in the field that you can seek out for guidance?
- Are there people (such as doctors, a family member, etc.) who should know about what you're doing?
- Do you need to hire anyone (such as a counselor or teacher) to help guide you on this journey?

Data Preparation

With any goal, it's important to get real about three things: where you currently are, where you want to be, and what it will take to get there. This is where data collection is so helpful. You can use data to determine how much effort you need to devote to your goal and to track your progress. For instance, I couldn't know how much to reduce my sugar consumption and how much to increase my vitamin intake without knowing my current readings. Data are even helpful for a breakup. You can consider how many days per week you are unhappy with your partner; if your unhappy days out-number the happy ones, perhaps it's time to call it off.

Here are some questions to answer about data collection:

- What are the quantitative aspects of your goal? What are the qualitative ones?
- Are there ways you can quantify certain aspects of your goal that you may not have thought of before?
- What are the statistics by which you will measure success of your goal?
- What statistics will you need to keep track of as you move toward your goal?

Financial Preparation

Just as data preparation tells you how far you have to go to reach your goal, financial preparation helps you figure out how much it will cost and how you will allocate funds. When I was getting healthy, I asked myself whether I wanted to set aside part of my budget for a trainer, a gym membership, new fitness classes, or a new doctor. For big life goals, like becoming a parent, financial preparation is even more important.

You might find that your goal is too expensive or that you don't have enough money on hand to dedicate to that goal. If this is the case, you may not need to initially invest in every aspect of meeting your goal. For instance, if improving your fitness level is your goal, could you spend money on a gym membership instead of a package of classes at a boutique Pilates studio? Maybe you don't hire a trainer right away and instead get a training app for your phone. Investing only the money you can afford will still get you one step closer to your goal.

Here are some questions to answer about your finances:

- How much do you want to spend on your goal?
- Where will you get the funds to finance your goal?
- If your budget is tight, can you source any essential items used or secondhand or borrow them from someone else?
- What major expenses will you incur? Are any of these expenses recurring? (For example, might you need to pay an upfront cost for a membership or service? Do you need to make monthly payments toward a class?)

Schedule Preparation

It sounds simple enough to allot a certain amount of time per day to reaching your goal, but oftentimes the reason people don't accomplish a goal is simply that they didn't make enough time to do so. Yes, life throws curveballs, and we are sometimes forced to adapt. But it's important to have a dedicated time every day for doing the things you absolutely want to do. To make that time, you might have to let go of some prior commitments, rearrange some activities, or rethink how you work. For instance, if you want to make it to that spin class, you may need to be vigilant about your schedule and dedicate the time to getting on that bike! To raise a child, you will need to make sure you have the time you need to go to the required doctor's visits, to take the parental leave, and to do pickups and drop-offs when the child is older.

Here are some questions to answer about your scheduling of time:

- How much time do you need to dedicate to your new goal? Will you dedicate time daily, weekly, or monthly?

- How will you make time for this new goal? Do you need to change your schedule or eliminate some activities to make room for it?
- Which aspects of your new goal are the most time-consuming?
- At what point do you want to reassess your schedule to see if you need to tweak or change so as to allot more or less time for it?

The Joy of Preparation

Preparation might sound like the tedious work, the unfun part of the journey that you have to do before getting to the exciting tasks. But it doesn't have to be that way. Think about the anticipation you get in planning a vacation. How exciting is it to pick your next destination by spinning the ol' globe or running a finger across a map with your eyes closed? Or to buy guidebooks, language tutorials, and travel magazines to educate yourself about your destination? Or, let's go way back—remember the excitement of planning for the first day of school? Remember how you felt when you shopped for those new school supplies or laid out that fresh first-day-of-school outfit?

If you find yourself slogging your way through Preparation, here are a few tips to get you excited about planning:

- **MAKE IT FUN!** Turn on your favorite tunes or playlist while you clean out your garage or sit down to plan your budget. Music can boost your mood, even when you're doing the most mundane work. If you need to buy special equipment, take some time to look through a catalog or spend an afternoon window shopping.
- **VISUALIZE THE END RESULT:** Envisioning the fruits of your labor will help make the work worth it. Take a few minutes to think about the endgame and how it will make you feel once you've accomplished your goal.
- **CREATE A BEAUTIFUL WORKSPACE:** Make your workspace a fun place to complete your tasks. Add some flowers to your desk

and pin a fun poster on your wall. Buy some colorful pens or eye-catching notebooks. Post pictures of inspiring places, spaces, quotes, or messages on a bulletin board. Eye candy can be a great motivator.

- **GAMIFY YOUR TASKS:** Turning your prep work into a game makes it more fun and incentivizes you to seek steady progress over time. Cleaning old gum wrappers and crumbs out of the back seat of your car may not be the most thrilling task, but if you treat it like a challenge in an obstacle course, it can become so!

Know Your Nonnegotiables

Our culture valorizes giving your all, or 110 percent of your effort, to everything. While that might be something you need to do in the short term, it's an untenable way to complete a long-term project. To prevent yourself from burning out and/or losing steam midway through the Elevation Approach, you'll need to decide what you're willing to give toward your goal and what you're not willing to give up.

Establishing these boundaries in the Preparation phase will set you up to work at a steady, sustainable clip toward your goal, preventing it from becoming all-consuming or burdensome. Even when things get tough or challenging, knowing these borders will remind you that you still have other needs to honor, and it will make it easier to know when to put something down. Because you set those boundaries in advance, you'll have guidelines to follow if you need to reevaluate your priorities; this helps you avoid making tough choices when you're feeling tired or overworked.

Before beginning any project, I always take a moment to determine my nonnegotiables—the things I refuse to set aside for work. (As you learned in chapter 1, a good night's sleep is on that list for me!) Here are the guidelines I use to make this list:

- **FIGURE OUT WHAT YOU'RE NOT WILLING TO SACRIFICE:** Your nonnegotiables are often the essential tasks in your life every day. For example, these may include certain family obligations you can't neglect or relaxing activities, such as a Saturday morning stroll with your dog, that anchor your day. Don't forget about your everyday needs, like regular mealtimes or, for some people, a daily green smoothie.

- **SET YOUR LIMITS:** Knowing when you do your best work allows you to organize your day efficiently and effectively. For example, if you know you're not a morning person, a 5:30 a.m. bootcamp class is not on your path to success; you'll have difficulty getting to the class, and you may not perform at your peak while there. Instead, make later start times for activities a nonnegotiable, and sign up for evening classes instead.

- **BUILD IN TIME FOR BREAKS:** Everyone needs breaks. Take a moment to rest so you don't overwhelm yourself. Also, build in an alternate time to complete a desired activity, should you need to take an unplanned break.

- **SET A BUDGET AND CREATE GUIDELINES FOR CHANGING IT:** For many of us, our budgets are one of our biggest nonnegotiables. After you establish the budget for your goal, go one step further and consider whether you have room to cover additional costs, should these costs be warranted. Having this structure will not only prevent you from spending more than you're comfortable with but also provide the parameters for spending more when necessary.

Exercise: Create Your Nonnegotiables List

Now, let's set up some guardrails so you can move forward without veering off the road on a curve. Use this exercise to create your list of nonnegotiables. Describe five things you will protect while you move toward your goal on the Elevation Approach.

1. _____

2. _____

3. _____

4. _____

5. _____

Troubleshooting: "Help, I'm Stuck!"

It's common to have doubts about your ability to start something new. We've all felt the pang of uncertainty that creeps in just before we're about to hit the Go button, especially if we've tried to get a plan going before and couldn't get it off the ground.

My tip for fighting that feeling of overwhelm is to first tackle one bite-sized task related to your goal. Completing just one small task will give you the gratification that comes with getting something done—it's a boost of confidence to help you move forward.

Suppose you're renovating that basement into a game room. There are many decisions to make. For example, you'll need to figure out where to buy furniture, to obtain and compare bids from contractors, to determine if your top choices will fit your budget, and to choose a design style that works for the space you envision. If this sounds like a lot of decisions to make, take a half hour to visit

> your hardware/paint store and pick up some paint swatches. The next day, spend another half hour selecting your favorite colors. Do one small task every day for a few weeks, and you'll have settled on a look for your game room, ready to take the next step.

I'm Ready. Now What?

As mentioned in chapter 2, there are three key principles for each phase of the Elevation Approach and these principles will guide you toward your goal. The three principles in the Preparation phase help you make space for the new tasks, ideas, and tools in your life.

The first principle is to **declutter your space**. You'll clean out old or unused goods and at the same time clear away your fears and worries.

The second principle is to **get curious**. You'll open yourself up to the possibility of reaching your goal. This will prevent you from talking yourself out of your big plan before it can even get started.

Then the third principle is to **know your numbers.** You'll get down to brass tacks and collect some real data for what you need. This is the best way to get real about where you are in life and what you need to get the things you want.

THREE QUESTIONS FOR PREPARATION

At the end of each phase, we'll think through a few questions to assess whether you're ready to move on to the next phase. When you've worked through each phase's three principles, you will be well prepared to take on whatever goal you have in mind. You'll know that you're ready to move on to Inspiration if you can answer yes to these three questions:

1. Have I created clutter-free physical and mental spaces, and a clear schedule to take on my goal?
2. Have I adopted a curiosity mindset about the great things that could happen if I reach my goal?
3. Have I analyzed the facts, figures, and costs of my goal, and do I feel prepared to continue gathering the data to track my progress?

CHAPTER 4

Principle #1: Declutter Your Spaces

Using the Elevation Approach to create work-life harmony and pursue your biggest goals will likely involve bringing new tasks, projects, and changes into your life. When you are doing something new, you need to make space for it—literally and figuratively.

As you prepare to reach for your big goal, your first thing to do is to welcome those future changes by decluttering. Decluttering is not just about aesthetics and putting things where they look best. It's also not about redecorating or painting over the messy parts of your home, nor does it mean creating a pretty Instagram-ready kitchen pantry.

Instead, decluttering is about clearing out the unnecessary things in your life to give yourself space to work on your goal, which then allows new energy and ideas to flow in, as well as makes more room for joy. Clearing away any physical or mental roadblocks is especially important at the beginning of the Elevation Approach, as it ensures you're creating an environment that supports the changes you want to make. By decluttering, you are sending a clear signal to the world (and yourself) that you are ready to start something new and can be trusted to complete the work toward your goal.

To help you get started, let's review what types of clutter we encounter in our lives, what that clutter is trying to tell you, and how best you can tackle the decluttering. You'll learn how to signal your readiness for something new by cleaning out the things that are old and unwanted in your life.

Types of Clutter

For me, clutter is any misplaced or unwanted item that creates negative feelings and prevents me from focusing on my tasks at hand. This definition is broad, but it helps you see how to apply it to your own situation. After all, what's clutter to one person may not be clutter to another; it all depends on circumstances and personal preferences.

So, clutter can take on many forms and can affect many aspects of our lives:

Physical clutter is the stuff we usually think of when we hear the word. It might be a lot of unworn clothes stuffed into a closet, or forgotten sports equipment and lawn ornaments piled up in a garage, or in the case of my kitchen counter, unopened flyers and used paper cups.

Mental clutter is the thoughts, worries, concerns, and desires that distract us and distress us.

Digital clutter is anything on our devices that overwhelms us. It can include long lists of emails, lengthy documents, received bills, unused apps, and hastily taken bad photos. Think about how many newsletters are in your inbox or all those digital news subscriptions you might be receiving.

Calendar clutter is the tasks, meetings, events, and other commitments that make us feel overscheduled.

Take a moment to inventory the clutter in your life. Do you have things in these categories that you can clear out? Is clutter taking up unwanted spaces in your life? Don't worry—we all have some clutter, somewhere. And don't worry that having some clutter means you're a messy person or that you'll permanently be a mess. Clutter is something that can be managed, and paying attention to it now can free you up to think about bigger challenges in your life.

Your Clutter Is a Sign

Clutter can be ugly, maddening, and just a plain pain in the butt. It can also affect, and reflect, how we feel about ourselves and our surroundings. Your clutter might be a signal that you need to make some changes in your circumstances to bring your work and life back into alignment.

Unwanted Clutter Reflects a Glitch in Your Systems

Clutter tells you that something in your life is not running as smoothly as possible. For instance, at a factory that sorts packages, when there's a problem with the system, it will result in a backup of packages. In our lives, a glitch in one of our systems sometimes results in clutter. That's why it's important to manage the clutter. Doing so gives you the chance to examine what's really going on in your life.

My kitchen's island countertop is the spot in my home where things from all parts of my life seem to land, whether bills and other mail to avocados, ring lights for video calls, and pretty flowers. It is a place where I work as well as eat. It is also where I prep food and sort my mail. But when my island countertop becomes cluttered, I begin to feel overwhelmed.

I can't tell you how many times I've felt anxious, only to realize my kitchen countertop was the cause. It took some time, but I realized that a cluttered kitchen countertop is my first sign that my work-life harmony is off. For example, right now that countertop is a MESS! I am leaving for a trip in two days and am hosting a party the day before I leave. It makes me aware that I am in a busy period and need to take some time to reset my priorities.

The state of my closet also serves as a cue that I'm not streamlining my wardrobe decisions. Constantly thinking about what to wear for my daily appointments, finding the items, and then giving them a fresh press takes a lot of energy and often leads to decision fatigue. The physical manifestation of this misspent energy is seeing my clothes and shoes strewn about the closet. In other words, the physical clutter mirrors the mental clutter I have about getting to my meetings, workouts, and get-togethers. Now, I take 30 to 40 minutes on Sundays to organize my clothes for the week. I put together the outfit for each event and I hang each one on a valet rack. This routine keeps my closet organized while allowing me more time on weekday mornings to make other decisions.

Listen to Your Clutter

Clutter might be a problem that seems to have an easy short-term fix, but that often isn't the best long-term solution. Your initial response to physical clutter might be to clean it up right away or shove it out of sight. Or, you might tackle calendar clutter by immediately canceling the plans you had for the weekend or block your fears and worries about them by ignoring the plans. While these solutions might work in the short term, they won't help you prevent that clutter from happening again.

Decluttering doesn't just involve tidying up. It also involves noticing the problem and fixing the glitch that caused it. Here are some long-term actions you can take to make that moment of desperation seem more useful:

1. **OBSERVE WHEN YOUR CLUTTER BEGINS TO BOTHER YOU.** Clutter often accumulates without attracting attention, but eventually there's a point when it becomes hard to ignore and you need to take action. That is what I call the "clutter trigger point." For me, having 1,000 emails in my inbox is a clutter trigger point. Or, if my kitchen countertop is so covered that I can't see the surface, that's another clutter trigger point: I know I can't ignore the mess. When does your clutter motivate you to take control?

2. **STOP! DON'T CLEAN UP THE CLUTTER IMMEDIATELY.** Instead, think about how that clutter makes you feel and take some time to understand why it accumulates.

3. **ASK YOURSELF WHY THE CLUTTER ACCUMULATED.** Consider how your clutter got to be as out of control as it is. What was going on in your life that made you too busy to deal with the clutter earlier? Are the conditions that created that clutter temporary or is there a long-standing issue at work? Knowing why clutter collects will make it easier to tackle the underlying reasons or identify other responsibilities that prevent you from dealing with it.

4. **THINK ABOUT WHAT YOU WANT TO SEE IN PLACE OF THE CLUTTER.** What things do you want to make room for? What feelings do you want to cultivate from a clutter-free space? Do you want to feel calmer? More creative? More like a leader?

The Rules of Decluttering

Now that you've learned what clutter is and why it deserves your attention, let's see how you can start decluttering.

Many a home renovation specialist or closet organizer has made millions performing this exercise for customers, but that doesn't mean you need an expert to tackle your closets or manage the apps on your devices. Decluttering is a simple, useful task to perform when the objects around you make you feel overwhelmed or anxious. Decluttering should give you a sense of peace and help you feel more "unstuck." When I sort through my inbox and get the number of emails down to a few hundred, I feel I've regained control over my correspondence—and life in general. My clean kitchen countertop makes me feel I can handle any roadblock. So, when you're getting started with a goal, let decluttering do the same for you, giving you that kick-start you need to bring more harmony into your life.

Here are a few simple rules to declutter your space. These rules also help focus your energy while you clean up. After all, it's easy to start cleaning a countertop, then all of a sudden move into deep-cleaning the garage, ultimately taking up way more time than you wanted to devote to this task. These rules help you keep your decluttering task manageable.

1. Start small and start short.

This is the most important rule for decluttering. When you begin, focus on a small area and dedicate a short amount of time to it. Starting small and working in short sessions can prevent you from feeling overwhelmed. Still engaged after the short amount of tidying? Keep going for another session.

Set a timer and tackle a bookcase shelf, the desktop in your office, or perhaps a kitchen cabinet. You can go even smaller. For example, start by cleaning out your purse. Dump out the loose change, the half-empty lipsticks, the old bottle of hand sanitizer, and any other useless items. Place back in your purse only those items you love and use daily.

2. Know how you want your space to feel.

When decluttering, create a clear vision for what you want your space to look and feel like when you're finished. This will help you figure out which items you need to retain in the space and which items don't fit the vibe you're trying to cultivate. For example, if you're decluttering an office, perhaps you want a workspace that makes you feel focused and alert. Or, want your mind to feel more relaxed? Set aside the stressful or worrisome thoughts, even if just for a few minutes. Do you want to feel less stressed when you check your inbox for messages? Figure out how many messages you can leave unread until you start to feel ill at ease. If you want your schedule to feel less harried, find out which meetings you can skip.

3. Find a home for your items.

Sometimes, the goods you consider clutter just need a new place to live. Your items may be useful but stored in the wrong place, or not useful to you but perhaps could be useful to someone else, or maybe they just need to be discarded. As you begin to clear your space, consider categorizing your things into these three groups: things you keep, things you donate, and things you toss. You can toss or keep the mental clutter, too.

For example, if you've got a big goal or task at hand, and you want your mind clear of distractions, toss out all the things unrelated to your task. Say you're interviewing for a new job, think about how to present your strengths or how to negotiate your target salary. Concerned about whether your high school crush follows you on Instagram? That's irrelevant for now, so toss that worry aside. Since you can't donate your mental clutter, try to delegate it—for instance, are you focusing on something that someone else can do much better? Assign that task to that person so you don't have to waste mental space on it.

4. Don't keep anything "just in case" you might need it.

People are tempted to hold on to things they no longer use because they think there is a chance they might need them one day. This mindset prevents you from making room for something new. Let me reassure you: you won't need it. Just let it go.

instant elevation with . . .

MICHELLE MORAGNE-MORRIS

Michelle Moragne-Morris has been a cleaning expert for over twenty-five years, as the founder of Squeeky Clean cleaning and decluttering service, located in New Jersey. She's also the mom of five kids. Here, she reveals why decluttering is essential for our lives, offers tips on how to do it well, and shares a foolproof method for creating a calm, beautiful space.

A cluttered space hinders your day from being as productive as it can be. Clutter also causes anxiety and keeps your brain from focusing on the task at hand. Your brain takes in all the sensory images around you—the good, the bad, and the ugly. If it's focusing on the clutter in your space, how can it focus on tasks? How can you start your day with a clear head? How can you listen to the voice of your creativity speaking over the sound of noise and clutter that is tuning it out?

Getting rid of clutter, creating a system that keeps the clutter away, and keeping your space organized is a step to being creative, being able to solve problems, and come up with new solutions for our lives. A clutter-free space creates harmony and balance for you and your mind. Here are some simple steps you can use when following the Rules of Decluttering (pages 57–59) to keep your workspace clutter free:

1. Keep your desk off-limits!

Your desk is the space on which you work, the place where you sit to begin your day and tackle your to-do list. One of the biggest problems I have seen is that some people focus on clearing their floor but leave piles of work, paper, and bills on their desk. This is a no-no! Your desk or worktable is supposed to be clear. It is *not* supposed to be a landing zone for your papers, mail, and items on your to-do list. Instead of using the top of your desk to store items, sticky notes, memos, or piles of "organized" papers that you'll get to later, consider dedicating a shelf, plastic bins, a credenza behind your desk, or file cabinets for these things. Sort the papers by category and place the ones you need during the day on the top of the pile. The goal is to create as much free space for your desk activities as possible, save for a few pictures of loved ones, flowers, and candy to offer daily inspiration.

2. Create landing zones for your things.

I have four bins in my office—one each for my bills, receipts, filing, and miscellaneous items—and small flat plastic containers in my drawers that hold my pencils, checks received from clients, note cards, and office supplies. Everything has a place. I set up this system because I do not have time to keep myself organized all week, and I don't want to see the clutter when I begin my next task or start my day. When you create your own landing zones, think of a setup that works best for you and your daily routine. Copying something you see on someone else's social media may not work for you. For example, you may be an artist who needs to paint daily. Will my bin system work for you? Probably not. You likely need lots of cups to hold brushes, pencils, and paints instead. Find a way to store your items in a way that can be both handy and easily concealed.

3. Put everything back in its place when you are finished working.
When I am finished working, I place everything back in its proper bin and shut the lid. The best way to start your morning is to be free of clutter, with no work staring at you from the night before. That avoids stressing yourself out before you even begin your task. Having a clear space gives you free moments to settle in at your own pace, plan your day, or begin your creative process. The more you practice this, the more second nature it will become.

4. Repeat these small steps to make a big impact!
Implementing these three steps will help you create a space that allows you to dream and create. If for some reason you get too busy and the clutter takes over, just go back and start again. The beauty of this process is that it helps you maintain your space at the level that works for you. These steps are not the overwhelming "purge your entire house" variety; rather, they are baby ones helping you develop a system that works for you moving forward.

Exercise: Declutter Your Physical Workspace

Blame complacency, small apartments, or just a tendency to over-buy and underuse, but people's physical spaces often get crowded with stuff. This excess can be just a hiccup we can manage. Here, you will clear away a space for the things that bring you joy.

1. **REMOVE THE ITEMS YOU DON'T NEED FOR REACHING YOUR GOAL.** For example, let's say you want to start painting, and you want to turn a small area of a room—or even a whole room—into a studio. Either way, make your painting space an area free of

debris, toys, and any other stuff not related to painting; set aside any items you can use for your hobby, such as paintbrushes or left-over paints.

2. CATEGORIZE YOUR UNNEEDED ITEMS. Enact decluttering rule no. 3 and get three bins. Designate one for items to keep, one for items to donate, and one for items to toss. Organize your goods into those three bins. For the items that you keep, find a new home for them based on their function. Discard the "toss" items. Give your donated items to family, friends, or a local shelter or non-profit. Schools are also a great place to donate old toys and books, and Habitat for Humanity and Salvation Army are great places for old furniture and blankets.

3. ARRANGE THE ITEMS YOU SET ASIDE. By now, you should be left with only the items related to your task. It's time to find permanent homes for these item in your workspace. For example, you might organize your paintbrushes using brush holders or cups. Store like items together in bins and organizers. Keep your workspaces as clear as possible. Hang any bags in a storage closet. Or, if you have nothing left that relates to your goal, take stock of what you need and begin to bring in those items. As you do, find a designated place for each item.

What to Declutter If You Have Only 5, 10, or 30 Minutes

Want to declutter a space but don't have much time to spare? Set your timer for 5, 10, or 30 minutes and tackle just a short decluttering project. Even cleaning up a small space can make you feel more at ease.

If you have **5 minutes,** declutter a bookshelf, purse, desk, nightstand, or makeup bag.

If you have **10 minutes,** declutter a kitchen counter, coffee table, dresser top, email inbox, or cellphone photo library.

If you have **30 minutes,** declutter a room, office, car, photo library, computer desktop folder, kitchen pantry, or hall closet.

Exercise: Declutter Your Mental Space

When my mind is overwhelmed, I can't think of doing anything else but solving my most pressing problem. For instance, I can't see how I could make time to cook dinner if I'm swamped with work and thinking about everything I have to do the next day.

Decluttering your mind gives you a break from thinking about a presentation, or the dirty dishes, or an upcoming renovation project. It lets you concentrate on preparing for that new goal. Letting go of worries, thoughts, or fears will help move you toward doing the things you really want to do.

A common way to set aside these feelings of stress is through meditation. Here is a super-accessible visual meditation exercise I call "boxing." It helps you clear your mind of worries or stress and asks you to imagine putting them in a proverbial box, then packing them away. This exercise is especially great if you're overwhelmed with racing thoughts or have just too many things on your mind.

1. Sit in a comfortable place with your back straight. Relax your body. Try not to be touching any objects that can restrict movement.
2. Close or relax your eyes. Take a few deep breaths. Think about how you want to feel in this moment. Do you want to feel relaxed? Calm? Focused?
3. Take one of the thoughts occupying your mind and visualize putting that thought into a box. Repeat with any other distracting thoughts.

4. Then pack up the box and move it outside of your mind.

5. When you're ready, open your eyes and gently begin to come back into your space.

At the end of this exercise, your mind should be relaxed and calm. You should now feel ready to take on your goal.

Exercise: Declutter Your Calendar

Decluttering your schedule will free up more time for the activities that bring you joy. The more joy you experience in your life, the more work-life harmony you'll achieve. Decluttering your calendar will also help you think more clearly and better strategize about making progress toward reaching your big goal.

So, if you think you can't find time for your goal, use this easy exercise to declutter your schedule. Here's an easy, step-by-step writing prompt to help you declutter your schedule:

1. Look at your calendar. Whether you use a digital calendar or an old-fashioned planner, analyze where in the days or weeks you are spending the most time and where you can lighten that load. Find opportunities to make more time for yourself and reaching your goal. For example, do you need to unsubscribe from some activities? Relieve yourself of some responsibilities? Share or delegate tasks with a friend to reserve more of your time?

2. Create a document on which you write down those activities you want to delegate or unsubscribe from. List each activity and figure out how much time it will save you each day or week. For example, if you don't want to pick up your child from school each day because fighting the traffic to get there leaves you stressed and often 5

minutes late for your 3:30 p.m. all-hands meeting at work, write that down. Be specific about how much time you gain by giving up this activity (in this example, 40 minutes of door-to-door travel time, plus the 5 minutes saved by getting to the meeting on time).

3. Decide which of these activities you want to eliminate from your calendar and which you want to keep. The activities that leave you feeling stressed or overwhelmed should be the first ones to go. See how you can either relieve yourself of the job or delegate it to another person.

4. For the next month, find 5 minutes each day to dedicate time to work on your big goal. Reserve this time for yourself, then see if you can up the amount of time after that first month. Maybe you can extend the 5 minutes to 10 or 15 minutes?

CHAPTER 5

Principle #2: Get Curious

If you want to consider the value and impact of curiosity on our lives, look to children, who are our best role models for this. They're constantly discovering something new and learning how things work. They interact with the world as if there were no rules or boundaries. To them, the world is new and exciting. They don't know their limits or even that limits exist. When they find out they can't do something or that something isn't good for them, they start asking questions.

And, boy, do they ask. They'll demand "Why?" over and over again. While the adults in the room might be exasperated, curiosity is how children get to know their world. They use it to discover possibilities, make connections between cause and effect, and learn how to move, grow, and think. From learning comes creativity, expression, language, and the ability to think and reason. Curiosity is key to a young person's development. Without curiosity, a child can't understand and explore the world around them.

Our curiosity wanes as we become adults. We grow jaded by the world's limits and obstacles. We quickly think about the reasons why we can't and shouldn't do something before we think about the benefits of giving it a try. We become beholden to our responsibilities and we are afraid of what will happen if we make a wrong move. *Will we be putting our family or our finances at risk? What will people think or say? Will we lose our self-respect or our hope if we try and fail?*

With this second principle of the Preparation phase, you rediscover the power of curiosity. Curiosity is an important fear-fighting and problem-solving tool, especially during this phase of the Elevation Approach. When you start something new, you might feel scared or out of your depth. Curiosity can help you stay positive and make you feel more confident about your ability to do the hard things.

Curiosity Leads to Possibility

When we're lost in the weeds of our everyday lives, it's hard to start something new. We might believe that we already have a good thing going and don't want to mess it up with a new plan or project. We immediately shut down another way of doing something because it seems too hard to implement. Sometimes we're so busy in our day-to-day rhythm that we forget to stop and wonder what else is possible.

If you have these doubts and uncertainties as you begin the Elevation Approach, then curiosity will help you look at the world with a sense of hope and opportunity. When you allow curiosity to guide your thinking, it will become easier to stay focused on the positive possibilities of your actions. Curiosity can encourage you to look beyond the familiar and help you support (or even discover) new passions.

When I was twenty-eight years old, I received my first invitation to join a nonprofit board. The invite felt like it was out of left field, but I had recently been profiled in the city paper and the piece caught the eye of a board member. I was brought on for my marketing expertise, and that was how I contributed the most.

It was easy to think of reasons to say no. I kept thinking, *Why do these people want me? And why in the world would I waste time doing this when my company was thriving?* Buzz Marketing Group (BMG) was now a top trendspotting business that had helped me pay my way through college and earned me recognition as one of the top young business entrepreneurs in the country. I had a client list of Fortune 500 companies. Being a board member would mean joining a team tasked with overseeing the organization's budget and giving approval for major decisions. I would need to find room in my schedule to attend the quarterly meetings.

I casually mentioned the offer to my brother, who was way more enthusiastic about the opportunity than I was.

This made me think. Why was I only considering the roadblocks? My curiosity had served me well in the past, and even helped me start my business. When I was sixteen, I loved pop culture. I responded to an ad in *Seventeen* magazine for a job at a newspaper for girls. I was hired to write product reviews on everything from makeup, to jewelry, to sneakers for companies like Saucony, Philosophy, and Dermalogica. I really thought I was living the life. When I'd send my reviews back to the company executives, they always asked me to write more reviews and sent me more products. I was in heaven.

After receiving my fair share of makeup and hair products, I figured out that companies were desperate to know more about young people and their tastes. I was a young person, and I knew a lot about young people. What if I researched trends popular with teens and tweens? What if I found a way to tell companies what young people wanted? What if they paid me for my work?

I decided to revisit the invitation with the same curiosity that helped me get BMG off the ground. What if the nonprofit wanted me on the board because I was young and a newcomer to the field? What if my experience on the board turned into something great? What if I met cool people on the board, and heck, what if one of them asked me to join another board? My brother and I laughed about the idea for a few days, and then I decided to take his advice and join the board.

Had I said no to that board position and not indulged my curiosity, I would never have gained the board experience. I also wouldn't have learned some valuable business lessons. Just as clutter is a sign that something is off with your day-to-day routine, curiosity is a sign that something might be worth your time and energy. Curiosity will help you look out for positive outcomes and move past potential barriers. You'll start thinking past the can't and the won't and think of the joyful outcomes instead.

Be Curious Even When Things Get Scary

Less than a year after I joined the board, I got a front-row seat for what I considered the worst-case scenario for a business at the time: the nonprofit needed to declare bankruptcy.

I quickly learned that the organization was in dire financial straits. A decline in ticket sales and donations and an increase in operational costs meant its operational funds were rapidly dwindling. Though the nonprofit had no long-term debt, it still needed to restructure and reorganize its finances, which a bankruptcy would presumably allow.

As if the bankruptcy prospect wasn't already scary enough, I also realized something else: when you take on the role of a board member, you become financially liable. In a meeting with the entire board, we were informed we would all be personally liable for the salaries of the employees if each of us didn't vote for the bankruptcy.

At twenty-eight years old I was being asked to make a decision that could affect my financial future and that of many others for years to come. I looked around the room. I was the youngest person on the board. I had never been on a board before. I had no experience with bankruptcy. But we all wanted to get to a solution that would be best for the nonprofit's future. So, I did what I thought would help guide me through this challenge: I started to ask questions.

"Attendance is down and costs are up. Do we think that's sustainable?" I asked about overhead, program costs, and salaries. As the meeting went on, it soon dawned on me that the people who I thought had more experience, knowledge, and resources than me had just as many questions as I did. They shared my concerns and wanted the same answers as I did.

When you're in an unfamiliar situation like this or are facing a big problem, it's easy to feel overwhelmed or believe you don't know what you're doing. You might think you're alone in your struggles and need to fend for yourself.

Your first instinct might be to freeze or dive headfirst into problem-solving mode, but my time with the nonprofit has made me believe in the power of curiosity. By asking questions, I could figure out what was really going on, define the problem, and outline possible solutions. It also made me feel less alone. My questions helped me discover that I had more in common with the other board members than I thought. And the more curious we all became about what was happening, the closer we all got toward finding a solution and creating a better future for the organization.

Curiosity can even make a worst-case scenario seem manageable. Oftentimes the worst thing that could happen isn't as disastrous as we think. I remember the day the nonprofit's attorney walked us through the bankruptcy proceedings. He explained the numbers and how the process would play out. I felt reassured, knowing this was what the bankruptcy was going to look and feel like. He said, "Here's what it's going to cost. And here's what it looks like on the other side." Having clarity gave all of us board members more resilience for the process.

Once the board understood the situation, we *all* started asking the right questions. We hired the proper support, and the organization didn't just survive the bankruptcy but also came back thriving. It was a group effort to get curious, to obtain the right info, and to climb out of a big mess and onto a steadier plane.

When I first joined the board, I didn't feel I had the adequate tools or training to handle a situation as tough as that, but curiosity was my antidote to fear. It gave me the bravery I needed to navigate the challenge and the confidence that I could do it again, if necessary.

How to Cultivate Curiosity

Curiosity is a muscle that we need to flex often. Luckily, we don't have to tackle a problem as huge as bankruptcy to flex this muscle. Here are a few ways you can cultivate curiosity in your everyday life:

- **ASK MORE QUESTIONS:** Be inquisitive about the world around you, especially when it comes to learning more about the everyday things you love. For example, when you're picking up your next coffee order at your local café, ask about their coffee beans. Or, if you love a local bakery's cinnamon bread, ask the staff what's in their recipe. These seem like small-talk questions, but they help you figure out why you gravitate to certain activities or experiences. Plus, they help you make a deeper connection with the people and places you interact with. These questions might even help you navigate a tricky situation or lead to insights you can use to reach your goal.

- **MOVE SLOWER:** Take more time to experience the things you do and give yourself room to explore your surroundings and be present in the moment. When you slow down, ponder how something came to be and let your imagination expand. For example, next time you're sitting in traffic, notice the cars next to you. Take in the small details of each car, like the size of its wheels or the color of the paint. What might be the name of the paint color—is it teal or cerulean? Are there any items around you that are similar colors?

- **TAKE A SECOND LOOK:** When you pay close attention to something, you begin to find things that spark your interest and ignite your creativity. These moments can help you notice details you might otherwise miss. This is especially true if you're tuning in to something to which you don't usually give a second thought.

- **LISTEN AND DIGEST:** So often we listen to people or things around us to get something in return, whether it's information or a chance to swoop in and solve a problem. In many of our conversations, our default setting is to think about how we might contribute to the discussion instead of just listening. See what happens when you sit back and just listen.

instant elevation with . . .

EVITA ROBINSON

Evita is the founder of Nomadness Travel Tribe, a groundbreaking online community for travelers of color. A lifelong lover of travel and a curator of wanderlust, here she shares how she has let curiosity guide her since childhood and how it helps her run her business today.

I'm a curious child who never grew up. I've always wanted to know the why and how behind everything. As a child I would come up with a hypothesis to explain how something worked and then ask myself, "Okay, what do I have to do to test this out?" For the longest time, I was fascinated with television and wanted to be on TV. I thought the only thing you had to do to be on TV was get behind it. I poured water into the back of our TV to see if the water showed up on-screen. I was hoping to prove that everything I saw on the screen was happening behind the screen. Instead, I busted one of our TV sets at a really young age.

I directed the curiosity that lingered in me so deeply as a child toward travel when I grew up. The benefits of curiosity are landing in a country in a place that I've never been to before and figuring it out. It's random run-ins with people from different countries, cultures, and backgrounds. It's being able to crack a beer open with them on a street corner in the middle of Johannesburg, South Africa, and form bonds and relationships that I end up carrying with me for the rest of my life.

Play, creativity, and being willing to ask questions and not know every answer fuel my business and the liveliness of it. One of my mentors told me my curiosity would serve me well in the next iteration of my business. I'm one of those people who, if there's something new happening in my company, I want to do it the first time with whoever is ultimately going to be responsible for it. I never want to have sections of my business where I couldn't tap in or help if needed.

I'm also curious about how the big things and the little things just function. As the CEO of Nomadness Travel Tribe, my curiosity has helped me build the international experiences we curate for our group trips and events. And it has also helped me behind the scenes. Because I like to know how everything works, I can tinker with any new business function a little bit to see if there's a way for us to customize it and specialize it for our business experience, be it on the front end or the back end. Curiosity is one of the biggest facets of my life. I'm very, very grateful for it, and I do my damnedest to make sure that I continue to cultivate it.

Exercise: Turn "I Can't" to "I'll Try"

Treating a new idea or opportunity with curiosity can help you brainstorm how to make it happen. Let's suppose someone asks you to join them on vacation. You might think of some obstacles to going on that trip. For instance, you'd have to carve out some time from work or school. You might have to find someone to watch the house or the kids. You would want to buy some new clothes, maybe some new swimsuits. Knowing this, your brain might go into automatic "I can't" mode. *I can't get the time off from work* or *I can't find a babysitter.*

You can help your brain consider more positive outcomes by reframing the tasks as those you can try to do. For example, *I can't get the time off from work* becomes *I'll try to get the time off from work.* Instead of *I can't find a babysitter*, say, *I'll try to find a babysitter.* Even saying the words *I'll try* out loud can make the tasks seem more approachable and putting that stellar vacation I'm sure you deserve so much within reach.

Here are a few ways you can practice that reframing:

1. Write down any obstacles that could prevent you from reaching your goal in the form of "I can't" or "I don't" statements (e.g., "I can't find the time for X"; "I don't know how to do Y").

2. Reframe those fears by swapping "I can't" or "I don't" for "I'll try." Think of real-life solutions for getting through the challenges you fear (e.g., "I will try to find the time"; "I will try to learn how to . . .").

Exercise: The "What If?" Game

Asking yourself "What if?" helps you harness your curiosity to fight doubt or negativity. This phrase can help you tap into future possibilities and remind you of your own strengths. I do this exercise all the time. When I write middle-grade fiction, I use this exercise to dream up all kinds of scenarios. Sometimes this practice seeps into my personal life! When I am spiraling out of control and worrying about how I'm going to get everything done on my to-do list, I stop and play the "What If" game. It calms me, showing me a path forward. It works for me every time.

Instead of assuming something will never work out, ask yourself, "What if it did?" (Or "What could I learn from trying anyway?") Before you take yourself out of the running, consider the possibility that everything will come together for you. Imagine that success is within your reach.

Set aside fifteen minutes for this exercise. Use the writing prompt to allow your mind to wander and think of five awesome things that could happen if you reach your goal. Describe each item, starting every sentence with the phrase "What if . . ."

Here's an example to get you started: If your goal is to apply to a dream job with a flexible schedule, you might respond to the prompt like this:

1. What if I'm more qualified for this position than I thought?
2. What if the company offered me the position?
3. What if my new boss agreed to let me work four days a week?
4. What if the extra day a week allowed me to spend more time volunteering?
5. What if the pay bump from this position means I can save for a big purchase?

Now, it's your turn.

1. What if _____?
2. What if _____?
3. What if _____?
4. What if _____?
5. What if _____?

After you're written down your five responses, keep going! See how many you can come up with!

CHAPTER 6

Principle #3: Know Your Numbers

No matter how big or small your goal, no preparation is complete if you haven't taken stock of the hard data supporting where you are now and where you want to go. In other words, you have to know your numbers.

Knowing your numbers is about gathering all the facts, figures, and statistics pertaining to your goal. I believe wholeheartedly that every aspect of our lives can be explained with some sort of data. As such, it is pertinent you know your numbers before you start any goal or task, whether big or small.

This principle is obvious when your goal is something like buying a house. You need to know how much the sellers are asking and how much you need to have in the bank for a down payment. Assuming you aren't going to pay for the house outright, you also need to know how much to borrow (the mortgage) and how much interest the bank will charge for the length of that mortgage. You'll also need to know how much house insurance costs, how much the closing costs are, how much property taxes will cost, and how much any renovations you desire will cost.

Knowing your numbers helps with nonfinancial goals, too. For instance, do you want to sleep more? You need to know how many hours, on average, you're sleeping now relative to how many you're hoping to sleep. Maybe you will wear a sleep tracker for several weeks to get the data, but without it you really can't make a plan for more shut-eye unless you know how many more hours to add.

When you know your numbers, you have undeniable, quantifiable data that can inform your steps toward your goal. This knowledge is particularly powerful when you're starting something new because it gives you the wisdom to take on that task. Knowledge also helps break large challenges into logical steps. The real facts and figures of your situation allow you to make wise decisions and gain the confidence to move forward, knowing your decisions are backed by hard data.

Numbers Tell the Truth

Whether you're at the outset of setting a goal or in the middle of working to achieve it, knowing your numbers gives you a candid snapshot of where you are and prevents you from moving on autopilot. I learned this the hard way.

When I was running Buzz Marketing Group, I reached a point where I could no longer grow the bottom line. I launched my business successfully on my own as a teenager, but BMG was too tied to me personally to grow any further. My story propelled the company, but it also stifled its growth. I did not feel I could charge more for my services (a big mistake!) because I thought I needed to remain competitive, so my business ended up costing me more than it was making. I also didn't understand the idea of paying myself first. So, while the company looked healthy on paper, my bank account did not.

At first, I couldn't figure out why this was. How was I not making more money? I had the best clients and the best projects, and lots of success. I turned to my financial numbers and quickly learned how much I didn't know.

I looked at our monthly costs and realized how exposed we were when clients didn't pay us within the thirty days (which happened often). One day, in between board meetings and other commitments, I finally looked at our books. It hit me: my business was in trouble. I was quoting fixed fees for our clients without accounting for the extra costs that would be incurred if the projects were postponed or were taken in a different direction. The numbers told the entire story of my unsustainable business model. The irony wasn't lost on me—I was a corporate CEO, I was serving on nonprofit and private company boards, and I was teaching an entrepreneurship course to high school seniors at the Wharton School, yet I had failed to understand my own numbers.

Once I realized BMG wasn't making enough money to keep its doors open, I used those numbers to find a solution. I saw that I was personally grossing enough revenue by writing books, giving talks, and creating content. In fact, content creation rather than product creation was what was making me good money. I started to think about how I could do more of that.

This led me to a big decision: I had to close my agency. This was a hard pill to swallow, but the data was clear as day. I had to be brutally honest about where my business was going and what the best decision would be.

Our numbers give us markers of progress, behavior, and trends to track, as well as red flags that signal a need to either stop doing something or pivot to something else. I don't know about you, but

I can talk myself into thinking something is great, so looking at your numbers will prevent you from sticking your head in the sand and unintentionally creating a life you don't want.

Yes, looking at the facts and figures of a situation can be terrifying. Oh, wait, I gained *how* much weight? I've only saved *how* much for retirement? This project isn't really over budget, right? But there's real freedom in knowing the facts about your status and holding yourself accountable. It empowers you to take effective steps toward reaching your goal. And these quantifiable steps will get you where you want to be.

Gathering Your Numbers

Whether it's a business or personal goal, I break it down into as many hard numbers as possible. Instead of saying to myself, *I don't feel vibrant,* I can face the hard truth: I have not done anything to make me feel vibrant today. I have to do one or two things to feel vibrant. Instead of making decisions based on what you think or how you feel, you have the data to point to and say, "I know this is happening," and act accordingly.

Here are the steps for breaking down a goal into actionable data:

- **QUANTIFY YOUR GOALS:** You've already named your goal in chapter 2, but drill down on it and describe it in a quantifiable way, using as many specific numbers or figures as possible. For example, instead of setting your goal to save money for a house, maybe decide to save for a 20 percent down payment on a house that costs $400,000. Or, if you want to learn a new language, set your sights on a quantifiable measure: I want to study 100 hours of French by the end of the year.

- **QUANTIFY THE ACTIONS NEEDED**: Think about ways you can quantify what needs to be done to reach your goal. Suppose your goal is to learn French. How will you dedicate those 100 hours to your studies before you ring in the new year? Can you attend a certain number of French classes or devote a certain number of hours toward study? For example: I want to spend one hour a day studying French.

- **QUANTIFY THE TOOLS OR GOODS NEEDED**: How can you quantify the goods or tools you'll need to reach your goal? If you want to learn to draw, how much will art classes cost? Again, let's look at those French lessons: Will you need two French immersion classes a week? Conversation meet-ups with a French speaker? A download of the Rosetta Stone software? Try to pinpoint the costs and frequency of the tools you'll need to get to your goal.

- **QUANTIFY WHAT SUCCESS IS**: If you want to save $50,000 for a house, success is when you've saved $50,000. If you want to save 20 percent for a down payment on a house, success is a percentage of the price of that house. Consider quantifying what success is for you in as specific terms as possible. For example, regarding the French lessons, does learning a language mean you can hold a conversation with a French speaker for ten minutes?

How to Quantify Qualitative Situations

Knowing your numbers also applies to any emotional aspects of your goals. Say you're planning a cross-country move. This move to a new city would improve your life in many ways. You'll live closer to your family and you can help your siblings take care of your aging parents. The climate suits you better (no more winter jackets!), too, and the new job you have lined up will be a leg up for your career. Still, you might feel stuck and have trouble searching the apartment listings. You might be thinking about how much you hate to leave your friends and you might be worried whether you'll be able to make new friends. Maybe you're frustrated about the fact that you need to leave now, just when you started to feel at home in your current situation.

Knowing your numbers can help put your plans into motion, especially when doing so requires you to make tough decisions. If there are aspects of your goal that are hard to quantify, try keeping a tally. For instance, how many days of the week are you excited about the move? How many days does the prospect of moving make you nervous or sad? Perhaps you can rate your feelings on a scale from 1 to 5, where 1 means you're feeling unsure and 5 means you're feeling great about the decision. To help calm your worries about rebuilding your social life, you might record the number of local events you attend each week and track the hours you currently spend with your friends. When the move is done and you're ready to explore your new neighborhood, you can use the data to help you build new social connections and find new favorite hangouts.

When you have gathered enough data points, you will be clear about the pros and cons of achieving your goal and will enjoy the peace of mind that comes with that decision, whether it's a cross-country move or staying put.

instant elevation with . . .

SHENEYA WILSON

Financial guru Sheneya Wilson is a certified public accountant, the founder of Fola Financial, and my amazing accountant for several years. Here, in this interview with her, she shares what numbers drive her biggest life and financial decisions.

What are the top numbers you seek out when you invest?
Investments are all about creating potential appreciation and profitability. Thus, the top numbers I seek out to make investment decisions are the total project cost and potential profitability. Knowing these two numbers allows investors to determine the project's ROI [return on investment], which is calculated by dividing the profit earned on an investment by its total cost. A high ROI indicates that you made an efficient investment, which typically leads to great appreciation and profit!

What data do you live by to make everyday decisions?
I pay great attention to all relevant data around me, which can include data as complex as the tax code and financial and business articles, or as simple as observing the simplicity of nature. I believe that gathering data from all aspects of life allows us to learn and understand the world and helps us become more equipped to make any decision more confidently.

How important are our personal stats?
I believe our personal stats are essential to living a harmonious life. Frequently assessing your personal stats on a physical, mental, emotional, and financial basis will allow you to continuously improve and evolve. For example, I track how many minutes I spend meditating or taking some time for myself during the day. I monitor my consumption: what food I eat or content I consume, and how it makes me feel. Of course, I'm also analyzing my financial statements to gain insight into how profitable my endeavors are and what I can do to earn more. The goal to knowing your stats is to

win in all areas and create the life you desire by doing what you love!

Exercise: Get Your Numbers

Knowing your numbers is all about gathering necessary data. Use this worksheet to track a data point that's central to your goal. In the boxes, record your daily stats, and add any notes or information about your data in the writing space below.

1. What data do you want to record?

_____

2. What is the target that you want to reach?

_____

□ 1	□ 2	□ 3	□ 4	□ 5
□ 6	□ 7	□ 8	□ 9	□ 10
□ 11	□ 12	□ 13	□ 14	□ 15

Notes: _____

_____

_____

PHASE TWO

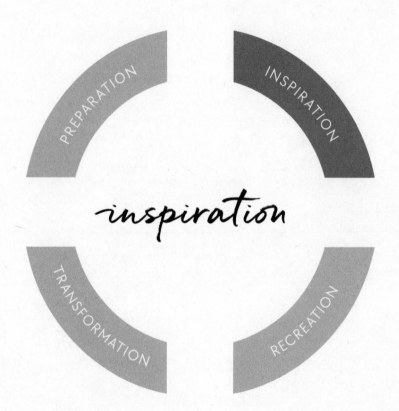

PREPARATION INSPIRATION TRANSFORMATION RECREATION

inspiration

CHAPTER 7

Inviting Inspiration

Traveling to far-off locales with new peoples, places, and experiences is certain to stir the imagination. But for me, it's the journey that sparks my creativity as often as the destination. I love people-watching, especially at airports. Although airports can be chaotic, I'm more relaxed and focused on my surroundings while I'm in transit. I observe what people are carrying with them. At the waiting area for my gate, there might be someone reading a book. A group of college students might be carrying sports equipment. I watch parents take out from their bags some toys, snacks, and headphones for their children. What are the other passengers wearing: Suits? Athleisure wear? Is anyone carrying a designer bag? Who is part of a family vacation and who is making a solo trip? What are other people's needs? Are they constantly running up to the gate agent or checking the schedule board?

When I was in youth marketing, I could always tell what trends were growing, based on my observations. I knew that Toms shoes was going to be a big brand when I saw three generations in a family—mom, daughter, and grandma—wearing their signature slip-ons. Same with UGGs. I could also sense that Away, the hip luggage start-up, was going to be big when I saw many of them among the carry-ons coming along the conveyor belt. I had lots of fun conversations with other passengers, comparing our bags.

This intel helped me pick out the products and brands that were resonating with young people. I could then study the type of marketing, language, promotions, and advertising being used and apply those insights to my projects at Buzz Marketing Group. Sometimes I used my notes to spark ideas for my writing. In fact, I've frequently been inspired to create blog posts or other content based on what I've seen during my travels. Some of my ideas for my middle-grade fiction series The Zee Files came out of my travels in London and Paris.

These stray observations have shown me how anything can spark an idea, a product, or a new way of doing something. After the Preparation phase, you've cleared your space, set your boundaries, gathered your tools, and collected some data. Now, it's time to move on to Inspiration—the phase of the Elevation Approach that helps you harness your powers of observation to stir your imagination. The Inspiration phase gives you hope and stretches your beliefs about what is possible in the world. It's the time to seek out new knowledge, listen to the people around you, and appreciate the wonders of your world, whether you're waiting for your flight to board or for a traffic light to turn green.

In this phase you learn how to find new ideas and use your observations to reach your goals. Since inspiration is best found when you're in the right mindset and environment, you'll also explore how to create and place yourself in those settings. You'll learn how to tune out distractions and tune in to the people, places, and activities that spark your creativity. You'll see firsthand just how big your ideas can be.

Find Your Sources of Inspiration

The Inspiration phase is an exercise in finding the beauty and novelty in our everyday lives. And that beauty can be found in a multitude of places:

- **ART**: Many forms of art, such as music, photography, architecture, or theater, may spark creativity by tapping into emotions or showing a new perspective on an idea or object. In some cases, art may invoke a feeling that you want to re-create in your own life.
- **POP CULTURE AND MEDIA**: From newspapers to music, movies and reality television, pop culture and its celebrities influence the way we dress, talk, and consider what's in or out.
- **PLACES**: Any place we spend time has an impact on our mind. From the familiar confines of home to faraway locations we travel to and explore, our surroundings impact our knowledge of our environment.
- **NATURE**: One of the most invigorating places, nature is a steady source of inspiration. To see how every being in nature, from tiny insects to large mammals, navigate its habitat can show us a new way to interact with our own world. As I mentioned in chapter 1, watching cheetahs and vultures share a meal in Africa was fascinating to me. Two animals so different yet so dependent on each other made me think about my close relationships with relatives and friends.

- **PEOPLE:** From friends and bosses to politicians and random people on the street, the people around us are a valuable source of inspiration. This is why I love people-watching during my travels. I also love meeting new people, especially those who have had different life experiences from me. I've had many conversations in which someone shares a gem of information that reshapes how I think about things. Or, someone can give a word of advice you didn't even know you needed! To make sure you don't miss anything, it's important to listen to another person's life experience and fully take in the speaker. And I mean take everything in, including speech patterns, clothing, and mannerisms. Be open to what someone else wants to share with you; for example, lean into those casual conversations you have when you're commuting instead of shutting yourself off by listening to your music.

- **EVERYDAY CHALLENGES:** Sometimes our day-to-day lives can be unexpected sources of inspiration. Many entrepreneurs have founded companies as a result of trying to solve a problem in their everyday life. For example, I founded my first company because I sensed businesses didn't understand what products teenagers like me really wanted. I was frustrated by how youth were represented in ads. This inspired me to think about other areas where I felt underrepresented, such as in fiction or even among women business owners. I often look to my own life for business opportunities. I ask myself whether something is a problem just for me, or if others have this problem also. I then use the opportunity to create the solution.

My Top Sources of Inspiration

I stay open to inspiration daily, but there are a few sources I turn to most often when I'm seeking those creative sparks:

1. CURATED NEWSFEEDS. Being intentional about how I keep up with the news helps me focus on the information I actually need to hear. Though not all news these days is good news, I choose to tune to certain apps and media outlets because they keep me current on topics affecting the entire world, without overloading me with chatter.

2. AUDIOBOOKS. I listen to everything from modern novels to fan-fiction book club picks. You'd be surprised how listening to a great novel gets your creative juices flowing.

3. CAREER NETWORKING SITES. I love apps like LinkedIn for keeping tabs on my friends and colleagues. It's also a great way to see how I can make deposits into their lives (see chapter 10 for more on deposits and withdrawals).

4. DIGITAL NOTEBOOKS. Taking notes on the go is the best way to capture your ideas, then organize them and put them into action.

Exercise: Inspiration Tracker

The people, places, and things around you can serve as not only a source of inspiration but also the motivational muscle to propel you toward your goal. With this exercise, you brainstorm where to seek out new ideas and inspirations. Write down some sources of inspiration you'd like to check out next to each listed category:

INSPIRATION CURATION

Art	
Pop Culture /Media	
Places	
Nature	
People	
Everyday Challenges	

Learn to Pay Attention

Sometimes it feels like inspiration strikes out of nowhere, but when you stop and think about it, you might soon realize that it comes most often when you're in the right state of mind. This may seem obvious, but between responsibilities at work and those at home, and the siren song of your digital devices, it might be challenging to observe, notice, and stay focused long enough to discover something new and exciting.

When I fly, I love the moment when the flight attendant comes by and asks us to turn off our phones. For me, it signals to my brain that it's time to tune out the notifications from my emails and texts and tune in to what I really want to do: watch episodes of *Bones* on the in-flight entertainment system or read a good book. No distractions, no responsibilities—these are the ideal conditions for creativity.

When I'm in this environment, I can notice things that I couldn't normally focus on. I even save certain tasks for my plane rides, knowing that I don't have access to Wi-Fi or phone service. During my last big trip, I reread a second pass of one of my children's books, *The Stitch Clique*, and after finishing, I immediately started working on an outline for the third book in that series.

You don't have to be flying to a far-flung location to find this environment, though. Many of our daily routines offer time-spaces when you can put away your distractions and sit still long enough to notice the world around you. You might find—and even create—the conditions conducive to inspiration while you're commuting to work, picking up your kids from school, or taking out the trash. Here's how:

- **STEP OUT OF YOUR ROUTINE:** Inspiration is often best found when you take yourself out of the places where you are busiest, such as your bustling workplace or a family-filled home where chores need to get done. But that doesn't mean that inspiration can't be found at work or at school, too. If you find yourself looking for that spark in these usually busy or chaotic places, try moving yourself to a new place within those confines. For example, while working from home, perhaps you can head to your kid's bedroom, just to look around and take in the colorful posters or melodic toys. At the office, you can go to a different floor to look outside the building from a different vantage point, or even appreciate a different office layout and decor.

- **DO ONE THING:** If you are doing many things at once, your mind will be too busy to manage the task in front of you while also staying attuned to the world around you. Focus on one activity at a time when you're looking for inspiration.

- **TAKE NOTES:** Recording something that catches your attention will help it stick in your mind. I always save the tidbits of inspiration in the Notes app on my phone or in a voice memo. If I don't choose to act on this inspiration in the moment, I can act on it a few weeks later. You can even go one step further and take a moment to reflect, writing down what comes to mind. For example, if you see a beautiful painting, don't just snap a picture of it or jot down the name of the piece and the artist. Describe the painting in your own words. Note what you like about it and what you want to remember. Because you took the time to reflect on the painting, it will be easier to refer to it later, and it will be one of the first things that will come to mind when you need a pretty image.

- **TURN YOUR DEVICES OFF:** Our digital devices can be a source of inspiration—plenty of apps on our phones help us tune in to ideas we've never seen before. But to tap into your own senses, you've got to put away those devices. Sit without your phone or television for a while and see what pops up. See what you can observe.

- **EMBRACE BOREDOM:** Instead of trying to fill your spare time with activities, allow yourself to be bored for a change. Leave the books and devices behind, and just . . . be. Focus on how the air smells. What colors do you see around you? Pay attention to what's going on. Listen to the sounds, the music, the words you hear. Allow your mind to wander a bit. What emotions come to you? What stirs inside you? What do your surroundings move you to want to do?

Exercise: Pay Attention!

The best way to learn (or relearn) how to pay attention is to practice paying attention. Put down this book, set a timer for 1 minute, and focus on your surroundings, noticing as many things as possible.

Then, for another minute, jot down everything you took in during those first 60 seconds: what noises you heard or didn't hear, what you or someone around you said, what colors you saw, what the air felt like, and what it felt like to be in that environment.

Lean into all five senses and see how well you can bring your surroundings to life.

Manage Your Inspiration

When we look for inspiration, we often seek out people who've had success doing the things we want to do. We read their books, follow their stories, subscribe to their podcasts, and emulate their processes. But there are times when the opinions of others influence us too much. When we're excited to learn new information and receive advice about our goals, we might become an info vacuum, sucking up everyone else's insights without taking the time to enjoy and focus on our own ideas. Sometimes insight can be *too* insightful.

In some cases, you might find yourself with lots of inspiration and not a clue about what to do next. For me, this is historically when I've gotten stuck. I've been so excited by something and am firing on all cylinders, but I'm getting nowhere. I realize that I can't figure out my next steps because I don't have a process for taking everything in and pinpointing the insights I need to refine my ideas. I am missing a critical review period.

So, it's important to avoid letting outside influences overshadow your own opinions or the excitement of this phase distract you from your own ambitions. Here are some ways you can rein yourself in as you open yourself up to new ideas:

- **YOU DON'T HAVE TO TAKE ADVICE OR OPINIONS FROM OTHERS, NO MATTER HOW WELL MEANING THEY ARE:** The most important opinion is yours. The loudest voice in the room should be yours. Don't let others drown you out. I can't tell you how often someone might call to tell me that my perfect job had opened up! I entertain the idea, thinking maybe I would be great at it, but I always turn down the offer when I ask myself whether this new role is the thing I am meant to do.
- **DON'T BE BEHOLDEN TO TRENDS:** Trends are temporary. What works for one project at one particular time may not be what you're looking for later. For example, if upgrading your work wardrobe is your goal, buying the latest trendiest fashions off the runways may not be what you need. Instead, perhaps classic, timeless pieces made with tailored fabrics that fit well and feel great would be better additions.
- **ASK YOURSELF, "HOW WOULD THIS ADVICE HELP ME?":** Asking this question will help you determine if the guidance you're receiving will help you advance toward your goal or point you in the wrong direction. For example, if you want

to become a better baker and you've browsed through baking cookbooks, ask yourself if one of the recipes you found will make you a better baker. Will it help you learn a new technique or give you the chance to try a new ingredient?

- **REMEMBER YOUR VISION AND FOCUS ON WHAT MATTERS MOST TO YOU:** If need be, revisit what you wrote on your SMART goal worksheet (see page 28) or review your vision statement (see page 41) to remind yourself why you're pursuing that goal and what you need to do to make that happen. Filter any inspiration you see through these lenses. It's great to be inspired by the basement renovations for a million-dollar home, but if your goal is to create a game room to enjoy more time with friends and family, you might not need that custom-made furniture or a professional designer to create a fun, cozy space.

- **EDIT YOUR SOURCES OF INSPIRATION:** Make sure your sources are aligned with what you want to achieve and how you want to feel. Many of us have followed social media accounts simply because they were pretty. But did they make us feel good? Did they teach us something? Did they inspire us to do better? While it's helpful to find inspiration in a wide range of places, the ideas you're consuming should help to improve your own life in some way. For example, parenting information on how to raise healthy children abounds on the internet. The feeds that offer helpful tips and images might be ones you want to follow. But those that shame children or their parents and use degrading language would be ones to avoid.

- **FOCUS ON THE FIRST STEP:** You may be looking for inspiration to tackle a big goal, but if you're feeling overwhelmed, turn your efforts toward resources that help you take those initial small steps and plan the rest later. Drink from your cup of inspiration in small sips, instead of gulping it all down at once.

- **REVIEW THE MESSAGES YOU'RE RECEIVING:** We are constantly taking in stimuli that impact our moods and motivation. It's important to be mindful to surround yourself with stimuli that lighten your moods, encourage you, and help you feel good. Consider something like your computer's log-in screen or your phone's screen saver. What is the opening image that you see? Can you change it to something that will put you in the right mood to receive new ideas?

Exercise: Conduct an Inspiration Audit

Earlier, I asked you to brainstorm ideas for gathering inspiration. Now, you're going to take stock of those points of interest to make sure the things you consume are inspiring and uplifting. This exercise will help you curate the images you look at, the books or texts you read, the news you consume, and the places you're visiting so that you can surround yourself with inspiration that fosters creativity.

You can conduct this type of audit at any point during the Elevation Approach, and I encourage you to do so regularly so you can edit your influences, keeping the ones that spark creativity and discarding the ones that don't. It's a useful activity to complete during phase two, but it's especially helpful anytime you're in a rut and feeling like something is off.

1. Gather the top sources where you look for new information and ideas. Include everything from social media, to magazines, to podcasts, to your role models.

You can write this information down in a list or collect the sources in a physical or digital folder.

2. Assess the information you're getting from each source. For example, when looking at a daily news source, think about the kind of information you're finding there. How do you feel after you've read a few articles? Do you feel more informed about the world around you, or do you feel a bit hopeless after taking in all the negative stories? As you assess your feelings about each source, sort these sources into three categories: inspiring, uninspiring, unwanted.

3. Examine your lists. If you find any sources in the unwanted or uninspiring categories, remove them. For example, consider a social media cleanse and unfollow those accounts or mute the people who are discouraging or distracting you from reaching your goal. Alternatively, if you realize you could use more fresh ideas on a certain subject, seek out a new podcast, newsletter, or media subscription.

Troubleshooting: "Help, I'm Stuck!"

Did you spend days pinning thousands of pretty pictures of home renovations to your Pinterest but have yet to buy a lamp, much less the rest of the furniture? Did you fill your bookshelf with baking cookbooks and your pantry with the ingredients, only to leave the books unopened and the sprinkles and chocolate chips languishing? If this sounds familiar, you might be dealing with inspiration overload.

I've experienced inspiration overload many times, and I've seen how it can turn into a serious setback if left unchecked. A few years back, when my marketing business was at its busiest, I was bouncing back and forth between the Preparation and the Inspiration phases. I would discover a new trend related to millennials, then try to design a campaign around it. Although I'd get excited about my plans, they usually fell flat. I quickly realized I had to stick with the process we've always used with our clients: collect the data first and then design a campaign around that data, not around the inspiration. For example, when Pinterest was popular, my first instinct was to design the entire campaign around this platform, but a more successful campaign would have incorporated Pinterest into a wider strategy.

Here are a few tips for preventing and/or managing inspiration overload:

- **CURATE YOUR SOURCES:** Instead of looking at every website, book, magazine, and social media account related to your goal, look at just three of them. For example, if renovating your home is your goal, limit the number of home improvement followers on your Instagram feed or focus on a particular style you like and use only the resources on that style. Instead of picking up every cookbook with "baking" in the title, focus on those with fast and easy recipes, especially if you're a beginner just getting to know your way around a whisk.

- **SET LIMITS WITH TIME BLOCKS:** Dedicate a specific amount of time to seek inspiration. For example, are you stuck on social media for hours each day? Give yourself a twenty-minute time block to spend on your favorite platform, then close the app.

- **SPLIT SOME OF YOUR WORK INTO TWO PARTS:** Sometimes the pressure to act on every bit of inspiration immediately can be overwhelming. Consider dividing this phase into two parts. The first part could involve gathering the inspiration, while the second part could be applying what you learned. For example, let's say you need to head to the library to check out some books for a class you've signed up for. In your first session, you focus on locating the books you need, and in your second session, you visit the library and flip through the books, absorb the information, and decide whether they are helpful.

- **PLAN HOW YOU'LL ACT ON YOUR INSPIRATION:** Figure out what you'll do with the inspiration once it strikes. Getting too caught up with watching a trend prevented me from successfully executing my ideas. Thinking about how your sources of inspiration will help you avoid getting overexcited, overworked, or, well, overloaded.

- **STOP!** When I reach inspiration overload, or a point where I am exhausted from ideating, the best solution is to stop. And guess what? That's what the next phase in the Elevation Approach is all about: Recreation. Sometimes, all you need is a break, which allows you to take a step back, take a breath, and recharge.

I'm Ready. Now What?

The three principles of the Inspiration phase help you find new ideas in new places, as well as show how you can manage that new information, advice, and ideas.

In the first principle you'll **create rituals**. Rituals are routine practices that offer you the opportunity to clear your mind, relax, and care about yourself with no interruptions. The more time you take for yourself, the more ready you'll be to assume a new task and keep moving toward your goal.

The next principle you'll practice is to **build a tribe**. You'll take a good hard look at the people around you and consider whether they are the right individuals to help you achieve your work-life harmony. If you're in need of new tribe members, you'll find out how to do that.

Finally, you'll learn how to **make deposits before you make withdrawals** in your relationships. When you are in this Inspiration phase, it's easy to take more from others than you can give, especially when you're asking the people around you for their time, energy, and wisdom. By giving before receiving, you'll keep those relationships balanced and avoid losing sight of your goals.

THREE QUESTIONS BEFORE YOU START

After working through these three principles of phase two, you might be full of new ideas and ready to move on to the next phase. You'll know you're ready for phase three, Recreation, if you can answer yes to these three questions:

1. Have I created a ritual for myself that is regular, routine, and sacred?
2. Have I formed a tribe of friends and family to provide help, guidance, and support?
3. Have I figured out how much of myself I will give to friends, family, and commitments? Do my deposits keep my relationships balanced and do I reserve enough energy so I can work toward my goal?

CHAPTER 8

Principle #4: Create Rituals

A few years ago, I read an article by design guru, television star, and bestselling author Joanna Gaines in her magazine *The Magnolia Journal*. She shared a fabulous recommendation: gather with your friends once a month and catch up over a bowl of soup, with members alternating as host. I thought this was a brilliant idea for my friends in Philly. While we loved spending time together, busy careers and family lives made it almost impossible to see one another regularly. So, I proposed planning monthly gatherings and trying this out for a few months.

My friends loved the suggestion—with one caveat. "We're in," they said, "but we don't want soup. We're going to do dinner." That was how our rotating supper club got its start. We've been going strong ever since, and we haven't missed a month. All eight of us have hosted at least one dinner in our respective homes. My friends are *really* great cooks, and everyone gets to showcase their menu-planning talents. We've enjoyed themed dinners, Friendsgivings, birthdays, and lazy summer evenings together. And the food is just part of the fun.

Our monthly ritual has also led to interesting dinner conversations. I'm lucky to have a diverse group of friends who can speak passionately about anything and everything. During our first dinner, two of my friends had a spirited and respectful debate about Israel and Palestine. Since then, we don't shy away from tough conversations or differing opinions on any topic—from the latest celebrity drama to our work. I've expanded my perspective, heard new ideas, and learned about experiences outside my own world.

The impact of this ritual has been profound. Knowing that I have one day each month when I am going to see my friends, hear about their adventures, and laugh for a few hours supports my mental health. I can let go of work stress or worrisome responsibilities and I can laugh, smile, and talk about practically anything with my always supportive friends. I come home from our monthly dinners feeling fulfilled emotionally and gastronomically.

Most important, this monthly ritual is part of how I achieve work-life harmony and stay open to new ideas. And with this principle you'll learn how to do the same by creating your own soul-soothing and emotionally nourishing rituals. The earlier principles of phase one helped you make space for your new goal, the possibilities that it can bring, and the work that it will require. Here, in this first principle of phase two, you'll continue making space, only this time around the space is just for you.

The Rewards of Rituals

A ritual is an activity or exercise that is personal, routine, and sacred to the person doing it. When people think of rituals, they often think of solemn, special, or in certain cases, holy or spiritual practices. But they don't have to be.

Rituals can take any form. Weekly manicures, cooking breakfast for yourself, walking the dog, drinking your favorite smoothie, brewing tea before bed, or playing the piano—all these activities can be rituals, as long as they bring you joy, improve your life, and are practiced for you, by you, and for no other reason than your own enjoyment.

Rituals are an essential for work-life harmony because they give you a time and a space to focus on yourself. They offer a chance to disconnect from the outside world and devote time to feeling centered and grounded. During this Inspiration phase of the Elevation Approach, you might take in exciting ideas, learn more about your goal, or discover new routines. It seems counterintuitive to take time to retreat and turn inward with a ritual, but doing so can help you be more receptive to the new and novel. Here's how even the simplest rituals can facilitate change and support your goals:

- **RITUALS CAN HELP YOU ENVISION WHAT YOU WANT TO BRING TO YOUR LIFE:** I use the time I set aside for a ritual to focus on myself and what I want to cultivate more of. My most important ritual is the ten minutes I spend each morning visualizing my day ahead. I let myself imagine the events and conversations I want to happen during the day. Sometimes I talk to God; sometimes He talks back. If I'm birthing a big idea, I think about what I want to bring to fruition. In those ten minutes, anything is possible for that day.
- **RITUALS CAN BRING YOU CALM:** The time you dedicate to your rituals can be spent in places or situations that are peaceful and calming. During a recent move, I decided I

couldn't part with my old coffee maker. There wasn't space for it in the kitchen, so I put it in my bedroom. Making a small coffee in my room has become my greatest pleasure. I don't have to leave my private space to start my morning, and I can stay in the blissful cocoon of my bedroom for a few minutes longer.

- **RITUALS CAN BRING YOU JOY:** Joy is one of the cornerstones of the Elevation Approach. The more joy you experience, the more elevated your life will be. By making time for rituals, you ensure that joy is a built-in feature of your everyday life, no matter how busy you might be.

- **RITUALS CAN BE A FORM OF SELF-CARE:** Rituals allow you to dedicate time to yourself and to the things that make you feel your best. Not only do they make you physically feel good, but they can meet your mental and spiritual needs as well. My skincare routine may take only three minutes, but it's the last bit of calm before the storm, or the time when I start my workday. I use products that not only feel good on my skin but also feel great for my soul because I'm supporting small businesses and the environment. For instance, I use products that reflect my values and purchase ones made by women and that use sustainably sourced ingredients.

- **RITUALS CAN CREATE A SAFE SPACE:** Rituals create a safe space to play, think, and just be. This sense of safety is especially important if I don't understand what's happening. The world can be overwhelming, the news can be devastating, and work or personal life might be hectic, but tapping into rituals can provide respite. For instance, when my father needed open-heart surgery, near his hospital in Lancaster, Pennsylvania, was a little coffee shop. After spending a few hours at my father's bedside, I would stop by the café to get a cup of coffee. This daily ritual gave me a break from the sterile surroundings of the hospital, so I could go back to my dad feeling refreshed and recharged. My visits to this café not only gave me the chance to have the best fresh-brewed, organic coffee in Lancaster, but it gave me time to clear my head, sit, and reflect—even if it was just for fifteen minutes.

- **RITUALS CAN HELP US KEEP GOING:** When you're making changes in your life, there's a part of your brain that resists those changes. That is, if we didn't have parts of ourselves that remain the same, our instinct would be to hold on to the familiar and that might slow us down. Rituals help us maintain momentum by offering a home base, where we can feel undistracted, comfortable, and relaxed. For example, one ritual that my sisters and I use as a home base to relax is our annual trips. We try to plan a few weekends each year when we're all together just to enjoy one another's company.

Guidelines for Great Rituals

Sometimes it can be challenging to identify a ritual that will work for you. If you need a place to start, here are some characteristics of rituals that will bring you more work-life harmony and support your search for inspiration:

1. **RITUALS ARE ROUTINE.** A ritual should be recurring. You can decide the cadence and frequency, but it should be something you do on a regular basis. For me, making coffee is a daily ritual. I take a luxurious bath at least once a week. And taking a solo trip is a ritual I do once or twice a year.

2. **RITUALS ARE JUST FOR YOU.** Your rituals should serve you and only you. This includes the rituals that involve social

gatherings. You don't have to describe your ritual or legitimize its existence to anyone. Do it because you love it. There's no better reason. I chat with my niece on Facetime every day, sometimes just for a minute, because she makes me laugh. And I read something for fun for ten minutes daily.

3. **RITUALS SHOULD NOT FEEL LIKE WORK.** Remember, rituals are a form of self-care. They should feel grounding, relaxing, and therapeutic. They should improve your state of being and bring you moments of calm, love, or laughter. If your ritual feels more like a chore or an obligation, you might need to think of another activity that's more soothing.

4. **RITUALS ARE DESIGNED WITH INTENTION.** Rituals should be activities to which you devote your full attention. Even something as simple as making a cup of tea before bed will be joyful when you can focus solely on your actions and the delight they bring to you.

5. **RITUALS DON'T HAVE TO BOOST PRODUCTIVITY.** Rituals should be about taking care of your needs, not about making progress or producing anything. If you look at food blogs and magazines every day because you enjoy gazing at photos of delicious dishes and finding new recipes to try, that's a ritual. Looking for recipes because you're in charge of dinner tonight? Not a ritual, especially if finding a last-minute dish creates stress!

6. **RITUALS CAN BE COMPLETELY UNRELATED TO YOUR GOAL.** Your ritual doesn't need to help you reach your goal or get you to accomplish anything related to it. In fact, these alternative types of rituals are encouraged. Think of rituals

as feel-good time-outs from your work and
responsibilities.

How to Create Soul-Soothing Rituals

I know we're all busy and can't always fathom doing anything for
ourselves, even if it's only for a few minutes. But we must. In fact,
I'm going to make it official, right here and now. You have permission to carve out time, space, and resources for yourself. Just for
you and your needs.

We've all been guilty of letting our own needs go by the wayside; if we continue doing that for too long, our own desires always
take a back seat. But here is your chance to prioritize what you
want and work toward getting it.

Rituals get you into the practice of dedicating precious time to
something that's strictly for you. If you get into the habit of, say,
making time to pamper yourself via a ritual, you will then get
comfortable making time for yourself to work on your personal
goals. The idea of making "me time" won't seem like an extraordinary event; rather, it will become a regular—and necessary—
practice, just like brushing your teeth.

To make rituals an essential part of your life, let's start by creating some. Here's what you'll need to do:

1. **SET ASIDE TIME.** Schedule time for your ritual and consider
   how you can make the ritual a recurring event. If you have
   trouble finding the time, start with five minutes, once a
   week. Build from there.
2. **SET ASIDE SPACE.** How much space do you want to dedicate
   for your ritual? A corner, the top of your dresser, or an
   entire room? No matter how large or how small your

space, keep it free of clutter and display visually soothing objects.

3. **SET ASIDE YOUR TOOLS.** Gather any items you need for your ritual and use them exclusively for that purpose. Reserving items for its exclusive use will emphasize the sacredness of your ritual. If you want to get into the habit of reading for ten minutes each day, dedicate a comfy chair and a fun bookmark just for this purpose. Want to meditate? A special meditation pillow or blanket will be a nice addition to your practice.

4. **SET ASIDE DISTRACTIONS.** Your ritual should get your full attention. When you're completing your ritual, get your mind to live in the moment. Fully immerse yourself in the ritual and focus on the task at hand, even if it's simply to relax. Let go of any worries, block off outside noise, and put aside any thoughts about work or responsibilities.

5. **SET ASIDE PERFECTION.** You'll reap the most benefit from your ritual if you practice it consistently. Consistency is much better than perfection. Remember, the main goal of any ritual, no matter what it is, is to leave you feeling good, and you can tap into that activity over and over again to consistently make you feel at peace.

instant elevation with . . .

HALLY BAYER

Hally Bayer is my Pilates teacher, the founder and owner of Thrive Pilates & Yoga, in Philadelphia, and offers on-demand Pilates and meditation classes at thrivewithhally.com. I've certainly felt centered and calm in her classes. In this interview, she shares with us how she's created a sense of peace for herself with some daily rituals.

How can rituals help us lead happier lives?

Rituals provide a sense of control and consistency that serves my health and well-being by offering me a sense of stability in an ever-changing and oftentimes scary world. My rituals provide me with a sense of control and consistency, helping me feel calm and grounded.

What rituals do you live by to bring harmony to your life?

If the first thing I do each morning is check my email, I start my day feeling anxious, overwhelmed, and stressed. So instead, I take ten minutes to meditate before I get out of bed, which makes me feel grounded, at ease, and ready to take on the day. My morning rituals continue with stretching, repeating affirmations, and drinking a green smoothie. In the afternoon, I text my dad my gratitude list. He texts me back his list. It's a great way for us to connect with each other. Every evening, I read to my son and then we meditate together before bed.

Can one have too many rituals?

I don't think it's possible to have too many rituals. I do think that holding too tightly to these rituals when they no longer serve us can be problematic. As humans, we are dynamic—we change, shift, and grow in different ways all the time. We have to be flexible in order to keep evolving.

Do you have any advice for readers who are carving out time for themselves?

If you're having trouble carving out time for yourself, I suggest prioritizing that time like you would an important meeting. It is actually *the* most important meeting you'll have all day. Rather than push it off or make it a reward for being productive, put it first—schedule it into your day as a nonnegotiable and build everything else around it.

Exercise: Design Your Own Ritual

Whether your ritual is a cup of coffee and journaling to kick off your day or tea and a face mask to end it, use these prompts to help you create your ritual and then dedicate a time and space to practice it.

1. Are there any activities you'd like to turn into a ritual? Make a list of three ideas that come to mind.
2. Think about how you want to feel during this activity. Do you want to feel completely relaxed? Do you want to feel creative?
3. Set aside a regular time in your schedule to complete this ritual. Is this going to be an activity you commit to doing once a day? Once a week? Once a month?
4. Decide where you want to practice your ritual. For example, if your ritual involves brewing a morning cup of coffee, do you enjoy it in a comfy spot in your home or take it outside?
5. Dive in and enjoy your ritual. After you've completed your ritual for the first time, write down any feelings or thoughts. What did you enjoy about your ritual?

To encourage you to enjoy your ritual as you practice it, here is a fun acronym—RITUAL—that is easy to remember. Each phrase offers a reminder to tune in to yourself and tune out distractions so you can enjoy your ritual and reap the benefits it provides.

You can tear out the following page and hang it wherever you want your ritual to take place.

The Rules of a Great Ritual

Your ritual should become routine; it is sacred and crafted for you and only you! Once you've selected your personal ritual, use this guide to set your intentions to feel good and be present in the moment while you partake in your ritual.

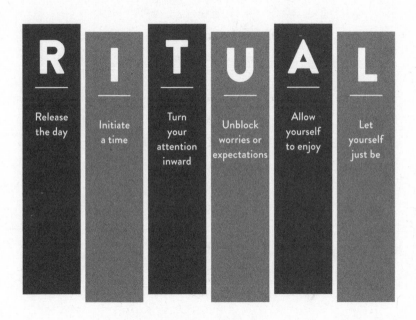

R Release the day

I Initiate a time

T Turn your attention inward

U Unblock worries or expectations

A Allow yourself to enjoy

L Let yourself just be

CHAPTER 9

Principle #5: Build Your Tribe

It's important to surround yourself with good people—people whom you can trust and whom you know will be in your life through the good and the bad. No matter if this kind of loyalty and honesty comes from family or friends, you need people in your life with whom you can share your big dreams and goals. These are the people who will cheer you on, help you out, or provide inspiration for you so you can reach higher, toward even bigger goals. And you'll do the same for them.

You can create this close-knit group among job or career contacts. Sometimes you can develop a support network among the people with whom you share hobbies or with whom you go to church.

I call my own support group "my tribe." They are people who meet the dictionary definition of the word *tribe*: They share with me the same language, customs, and beliefs. My tribe consists mostly of old friends. I have known them for years, and through career changes, marriages, divorces, babies, and moves across the country (and the world). These are people who inspire me, who bring joy to my life, and who have supported me through thick and thin. These are the people I call to help me solve problems, think through new ideas, swap recipes, and share travel tips.

In this chapter, you will learn how to form a tribe that supports you, in the process building and maintaining relationships with the important people in your life. When you surround yourself with people who align with both your life values and the effort you put forth into that relationship, you will find harmony in your relationships. Harmony in your relationships equals harmony in your life.

The Benefits of Building a Tribe

There are valuable benefits that you gain from building a supportive tribe:

TRIBES CAN HELP YOU FIND CONNECTION: Research has shown that social connection is key to personal happiness. Connecting with others brings joy and boosts physical health and overall well-being. For example, say you've moved to a new state to take care of an elderly parent. You may not have friends in your new town, which might make you feel isolated. Building a tribe in that new town will help you settle into the community and provide support for others who may be caring for someone as well.

TRIBES CAN HELP YOU MANAGE OTHER RELATIONSHIPS: We often feel overwhelmed by our obligations to other people. You may give a lot of yourself to one friend, only to realize that the friend hasn't been offering the same support to you. Mapping out your relationships and seeing how they interact help you see how you all share your time and knowledge with one another. It can also help you determine which people claim most of your energy and review what they are giving you in return. (We talk about how you can use this information to manage your relationships in chapter 10.)

TRIBES CAN BE A SOURCE OF INSPIRATION: In the Inspiration phase of the Elevation Approach, the people around you can help you move forward with your goal by bringing you new ideas and perspectives. They may serve as role models or influence how you see the world, opening your mind to new possibilities or offering creative solutions to the challenges you face.

The Roles Played by Your Tribe Members

If you look at your network of friends and family, you'll probably find that these relationships depend on what your connection is and where you are in your life. Some people come into your life for a particular reason; others stay there forever. The length of a relationship doesn't determine its quality, but knowing how each relationship enriches your life is the first step toward creating more fulfilling bonds.

It's important, therefore, to take stock of the people in your life and see what roles they play. Perhaps you consider just a few to be close friends, maybe because they have decades-long familiarity with how you've lived and what you've been through. Maybe other friends are more in the nature of social acquaintances, people you call when you're looking for restaurant recommendations or funny jokes, say. It's okay if certain people serve only one or two functions, while others serve several. Having a sense of how people figure in your life will help you not only better manage those relationships but manage your expectations of what help you can receive from them.

Many of the relationships I have with my tribe members fall into the following four categories. Use this as a guide to review and categorize the members of your tribe—or make up a few new categories, as seems appropriate.

Cheerleaders

Cheerleaders are people who give you praise and encouragement. They help you celebrate your work achievements and lend their support if you're experiencing a setback. For me, these people are casual friends and acquaintances. For example, I have tons of cheerleaders who like my Instagram posts or wish me a happy birthday on Facebook. And I love that feedback and good cheer! That said, these are not people whom I likely would mobilize to help me in a time of crisis. While my cheerleaders provide a nice boost of positivity, I turn to others when I need to solve a problem or seek advice.

Friendtors

Mentorship can sometimes be a mutually beneficial relationship, but that's not the traditional dynamic. Generally, the mentor gives support and information and the mentee receives it. That's why I prefer the term *friendtors*. These friendtor relationships are a step closer to those with your cheerleaders. Friendtors are peers and colleagues, and perhaps family members. They are peer to peer, with equal exchanges of time, attention, and guidance. These are people who are *both* friends and mentors, mutually committed to showing up for one another.

The Mutually Beneficial Power of Friendtors!

I hate networking, and I strongly dislike the culture around traditional mentorship. This might be a surprising confession from someone who has worked in business for many years, but traditional ideas concerning mentorship have left me feeling less than fulfilled. As a mentee, I sensed I was making too many withdrawals and not enough deposits to my mentor. My mentor–mentee relationships never produced the feeling of harmony I needed. I was always chasing my mentors, asking them questions or needing something from them, when what I really wanted was a relationship in which I was giving and receiving equally.

I don't believe people are "things" to be collected. We are not our jobs. The idea that we add value to someone else because we have a certain title is awful. The mentee is encouraged to put personal needs first and focus on what can be learned from the mentor, which doesn't usually result in a mutually fulfilling conversation, much less a long-lasting partnership.

Now, I'd be lying if I said I didn't mentor. But what's so beautiful about my mentor relationships is that in these relationships I, too, feel fulfilled. I can ask just as many questions and learn just as much from friendtors as they do from me. These harmonious relationships are the ones we both want to maintain.

Friendtors have kept me from making major career mistakes because they've challenged how I see the world. They've also rallied around me when I've needed help. They've advised me on my biggest leaps. And, more important, they've honestly just been good friends. And, probably most important of all, I just really, really like them.

Board of Directors

Several business leaders, including my friend Carolyn Everson (who you'll hear more from later in this chapter on page 127), talk about the importance of having your own "board of directors." Just as companies have a board of directors to oversee their operations, you should have a group of people to counsel you on major life decisions. These are people who have experience and expertise that you don't have. Your board should include a diverse and select group of people who can give you actionable advice to problem-solve. Your board members should not feel the need to compete with you. (After all, they might have already been where you're trying to go, so they don't see you as competition.)

Your board of directors are also your protectors. They're your elder statespeople, the ones who can tell you, "Here's how we fix this." For example, if you've lost your job, they might be pulling strings to get you a new job—calling friends of friends and connecting you immediately. They're the ones providing real solutions to your real problems.

These people are also the friends who challenge your decisions the most. For me, these people ask the tough questions that make me ask myself the tough questions. My board of directors is hands-down the reason I grow. They don't let me off the hook just because they're committed to helping me.

Fab Five

These are your closest of closest friends and family. When things are really going downhill, when everything awful is hitting the fan, these are the people I call. My Fab Five comprises my three sisters and two close friends. These are, as the kids say, my "ride or die" folks, the people there for me no matter what is happening, who know what I need, and never expect anything in return.

When you are in a crisis—and we will *all* be in a crisis at some point in life—you don't want to share your troubles repeatedly with a lot of people and consequently get a lot of different advice. You would end up in analysis paralysis, unable to come to a solution because you're overthinking a problem. When you need to withdraw for a bit, it's easier to do that when you have a small group of people who serve as your confidantes.

Your Fab Five will support you. They will hold you. They will listen to you. They will help you solve your problems, not always by providing a solution but more often by letting you feel your feelings and be completely honest about them. You can ugly-cry with these friends. You can react in ways you never would in public. They won't judge you, and they won't tell.

My best friend Missy is most certainly one of my Fab Five. I've known her since I was ten years old. She knows my family and all my deepest secrets.

Several years ago, I was deeply unhappy. Part of my unhappiness came from my decision to close Buzz Marketing Group, but this sadness went deeper, and I couldn't explain why. At a lunch date with Missy, I started crying, right there at the restaurant table. As close as Missy and I have always been, I'd never cried in front of her before. She may have been a little stunned, but she didn't miss a beat. She didn't advise me to "get up and get at 'em," as someone less close to me might have done. Instead, she gave me advice that surprised me. "Tina," she said, "you're so used to bouncing back. Right now, if you need to be down, why don't you just stay down for a moment?"

This was such a gift: she gave me permission to stay where I was. She let me know it was fine to just process what I was feeling. That comfort and advice could come only from someone who was in my Fab Five, a friend who had known me for years and years, and who understood how I processed my emotions.

Find Witnesses to Your Life

Some members of your Fab Five may also be witnesses to your life. These people experience life alongside you and support you through all the good, bad, and everything in between that comes your way. When we are younger, we often have more witnesses to our lives, usually in the form of caregivers, like our parents, grandparents, and other family members. We have teachers, counselors, and our classmates, too. But as we get older, these relationships are harder to find, and the number of witnesses becomes smaller. We're usually no longer living with our family, so we have fewer people to see us navigating the ups and downs of life. We're not in school, so we don't have a network of teachers or students to be our stewards and advocates. Though spouses are often many people's witnesses, as portrayed in the movie *Shall We Dance*, not everyone gets married.

Having few witnesses in your life should not be a cause for alarm, though. When it comes to witnesses—and close relationships in general—quality is better than quantity. (We discuss this in more detail on page 126.) Take me, for example. I am a single forty-something woman, and I have been single for more of my adult life than I have been coupled. I'm part of a generation for whom marriage may not be the highest priority. This doesn't mean that I don't have life witnesses.

My close friends and family have come to play this role. I lean on my tribe, especially my Fab Five, much more now than ever before. I've built a community that allows me to feel "seen." For instance, my very best friends are not the primary people who help me advance my career, but they remember moments that happened ten years ago. I treasure them, because they have accepted every version of me. While I don't always see them often, they are my through lines and they tether me to the story of my life. While making new connections is wonderful, I'm in it for the long haul with these friends.

Even if you are one half of a couple, you should still maintain strong relationships with your life witnesses. My parents have been married for more than forty years; I think my parents' relationship is thriving because they both have strong groups of friends. In fact, their closest friendships go back five decades—my mom's in her mid-sixties, my dad in his early seventies. These friends have become witnesses to their lives (and, by proxy, their children's lives). Witnesses, along with other members of your tribe, allow your personal relationships to thrive, because you're not relying on just one person as sole source of anything and everything for you.

How to Identify Tribe-Worthy Friends and Family

Relationships, especially friendships, get harder to keep and maintain as we age and have more personal commitments. As we spend more time with work and family, people who are not directly related to those things are often sidelined. Whether you want to make new friends or reconnect with people with whom you've lost touch, you need to make the effort to look for them.

Seek Out People Working Toward Similar Goals

I met some of my tribe members when I volunteered for community organizations and we planned fun events together. Specifically, we were there to create a lovely event for the youngest patrons of a local museum, but our friendships lasted long after the event and endure. I have met other tribe members through work events and others through friends of friends.

Charity organizations and hobbies are great places to find new tribe members. Is your goal to run a marathon? Are you interested in running for a good cause? Marathons are full of like-minded people with a common goal and interest—running! Do you go to the same place for lunch every day? Is there another regular customer there that you see every day? Perhaps there are some potential tribe members who visit your local haunts?

My point is that you sometimes don't have to look too far to find new friends—just do what you love to do and you'll meet people with the same interest.

Seek Out People with Similar Values

Of course, not all my tribe members have the same goals as I have. Some of my best friends are stay-at-home moms, which means our daily to-do lists are different. And yet we share some life goals—to find more joy in life and to spend more time with family. In this regard, we are moving in the same direction. We see the same possibilities, and we want our lives to be better. We love and support one another, and just try to enjoy our time together. When things are bad, we're there for one another—no questions asked.

Seek Out People When You're Trying Something New

Whether you're trying a new hobby or taking a solo vacation for the first time, you'll meet new people and have new conversations. Classes or adult education centers are great places to start. I met a great group of people when I decided to take French classes.

Seek Out People Who Are Different from You

It's important to include a diversity of experiences and a diversity of thought in your group. So often we think about building a squad of peers, but surrounding yourself with people who are exactly like you can mean missing out on different perspectives and ideas.

For example, my niece, Phoebe, who is thirteen years old, is an important tribe member. I appreciate hearing how she experiences a situation and comparing her interpretation of it with mine. We middle-aged adults have prejudices and preconceived notions that younger, fresh-eyed people don't have. Likewise, my older family members may have been where I am now and have yet another way of seeing things.

Nurture Your Relationships

Now that you have identified your tribe members, you need to cultivate these relationships. The key is to connect in genuine, meaningful ways and present your whole self. Here are some easy ways to help create connections between you and your tribe.

- **CONNECT FOR NO REASON**: Reach out to people, especially when you don't need anything. Say hello. Share a photo or joke that reminds you of them. Reaching out simply because you want to connect shows people that you genuinely have an interest in spending time with them, or that you're interested in cultivating shared experiences, even if it's just laughing at the same joke!

- **SHOW UP FOR THE BIG STUFF**: Birthdays, weddings, and funerals are key events in people's lives when your support will be noted and appreciated. Celebrate life events by accepting invitations or sending a short note to let that person know you're thinking of them on an important day.

- **SHARE RELEVANT INFORMATION**: Help the people in your life by telling them about events, activities, and resources they might find useful. For example, if there's a sale at a store you know your friend likes, forward the flyer. Find a recipe that's fast, delicious, and great for a group? Pass it along to your friend who cooks dinner for her family of six every night.

- **OFFER A SERVICE:** Everyone loves to be pampered, but nothing feels more personal than being pampered by someone they love. If you offer services—massages, baby-sitting, dog walking—consider giving them to a friend who could benefit from it. If not, treat that someone special to a service you know they would enjoy—even if it's just gaining some time to be alone while someone else walks the dog.

- **MAKE DATES:** Dates don't have to be reserved for your romantic connections. Plan dates with your friends and family to enjoy time to connect and hang out. This will also give you the opportunity to discuss a topic together. For example, schedule an afternoon to go to a wine tasting, check out a museum exhibit, or bake cookies for the holidays. If your friends live far away, phone dates are a great way to keep in touch.

Quality over Quantity

Meeting new people and exposing ourselves to those who inspire us is a great thing. And having a variety of tribe members in our lives keeps us evolving as people. But in order to not commit ourselves to friendships that don't bring us joy, we need to be careful about who we let into our tribe. I'm going to be really blunt here: not everyone needs to be your friend.

You don't need to include in your tribe everyone with whom you spend time. And you don't need to form a separate tribe for each interest in your life. I know a lot of people who are great associates, and I really enjoy my time with them. But I do not have the same close relationships with casual acquaintances that I do with my close tribe members. I do not put the same resources into those relationships as I do to my deep friendships.

Too many of us try to be friends with too many people. The result is we end up without any deep relationships and have a wide network of casual social connections. Your closest relationships should be with the people you can rely on no matter what, whereas your casual connections are often temporary or not solid enough to withstand challenges. Because you have only so much energy to put into your relationships, you need to prioritize those that are most important. We make commitments to people when we give them important roles in our life, so be discerning about whom you welcome into your tribe.

I don't have many deep female friendships because I have three younger sisters with whom I'm extremely close. While I maintain strong ties with my friends from childhood and my twenties, I prioritize my relationships with my sisters. If my sister asks me to come to Maryland and take care of her daughter, Phoebe, I do it, no matter what else is on my calendar. And I know she would do the same for me, because she already has. I used to travel at least half the year, and my sister would always go to my house to make sure everything was running just fine.

instant elevation with . . .

CAROLYN EVERSON

Carolyn Everson is a tech industry executive with more than twenty-five years' experience running teams at top firms, including Facebook and Microsoft. She was most recently president of Instacart. She's also a wife, a mom to twin girls, and a stepmom to two boys. Here, Carolyn shares how she nurtures strong connections.

Your personal relationships fuel a healthy life—physically, spiritually, mentally, and emotionally. Managing your relationships can sometimes be overwhelming, especially if you meet many amazing individuals throughout your life. I visualize my relationships as concentric circles I have built over the course of my life. I organize the people in my life based on the context in which I met them.

At the center of my concentric circles are my closest relationships—those I have with my family. We plan one or two annual get-togethers so that everyone can see one another and catch up. I also have three childhood friends with whom I am still incredibly close. Even after forty years, I reach out to them when I need someone who has known me for a long time.

I've created tight circles of friends based on where I've lived. When my husband and I moved to Montclair, New Jersey, over twenty years ago, it took almost two years to build a community there. We nurtured friendships with rituals and small impromptu moments. We hosted Memorial Day, Fourth of July, and Labor Day parties every summer at our home, and we would casually drop by to share a pizza and a glass of wine during the week. To this day, we consider many of the people we met in Montclair our best friends.

My next concentric circles include people from school and work. I have the best friends and sorority sisters I met at Villanova, where I went for undergraduate work. I have friends from my time at Harvard Business School. I'm part of the alumni networks for the companies where I worked prior. Sometimes, I call on my Sisterhood, which is the name of the text group I have with six women whom I've met in a professional context. We interact with one another daily, sharing personal updates, getting advice about careers, and comparing notes on raising children. They have become like family.

I have formed some of my strongest networks later in my life. My Henry Crown network, of which Tina is a part, has a strict code of confidentiality, and, as a result, I reach out to this network first when I am contemplating a major career move. I belong to another group of women called the Force Multipliers. I started this group with a close work friend, and we organize frequent video meetings and have an active WhatsApp group.

One of my most critical groups is my board of directors. I read a book a long time ago by an old McKinsey consultant who asked, "If companies have boards, why don't people?" I've compiled a group of people with diverse backgrounds and points of view, and they have been there for me during my toughest professional decisions.

My advice for building tribes is to think about the institutions and organizing mechanisms that have brought people into your life. You can often form tribes based on institutions of which you've been a member, such as the place you work, where you went to school, or the church or synagogue you attend. Maybe you can organize an alumni network from your first job if no one else has done so. Or try creating your network based on your location, as my husband and I did in New Jersey.

After you create lists of people based on the important institutions and times in your life, send a text or email to everyone in the group. Say, "Hey, I've been thinking about it, we had something special when we were together, and I'd like to keep in touch." You can even host an in-person event.

Exercise: Tribe Tree

Have you ever taken the time to map your social connections? Creating a visual representation of your support network is a great way to see how extensive it is and will show you where you can make room for more people.

This worksheet sets up a family-tree-style bracket system for grouping four different types of tribe members. It also leaves room to include your own categories, depending on who you have in your life and what purposes they serve for you.

Write your name in the gray box in the diagram. In the boxes branching off this diagram, fill in the names of family members, friends, colleagues, and acquaintances and note the roles they play in your life. It's possible that one person may play several roles, and that's okay.

CHAPTER 10

Principle #6: Make Deposits Before Withdrawals

At the bank, we make basically two transactions: deposits and withdrawals. We can't make withdrawals unless we have the funds in our account. So, to maintain our balance, we must make deposits that are equal to or greater than our withdrawals.

This basic construct of banking is key to managing your finances, and also key to managing the time and energy you spend on the people around you, especially when using the Elevation Approach. In the Inspiration phase, it's easy to get caught up in the excitement of learning, observing, and collecting new information. We call up friends for their input on the latest ideas, we take notes, and then we run off to complete the tasks. In short, we make connections with others without pausing to think about what we can offer them in return. When I'm ideating in the Inspiration phase, I sometimes am so laser-focused on what I need that I forget there's a person on the other side of the exchange.

On the other hand, we might find ourselves putting more energy into a relationship than we're receiving in return, leaving us feeling depleted or at the very least disappointed. We might over-extend ourselves and commit to too many obligations. We might feel we're giving too much to others at the expense of progressing toward our goal.

This third principle of phase two asks you to do some relationship accounting. In essence, you'll learn how to make sure your deposits match your withdrawals. By being more mindful of what you give and what you receive from others, you can ensure you are putting your efforts toward the most meaningful parts—and people—in your life.

What Are These Deposits and Withdrawals?

A *deposit* occurs when you give time, energy, love, or information to someone else. A *withdrawal* occurs when you receive time, energy, love, or information from someone else. Deposits and withdrawals can take many guises, whether as advice, favors, emotional support, or a token of appreciation, such as a thank-you note.

For example, you may make a deposit into a friendship by offering your friend some advice about a problem at work, after going through a similar experience. The next week, you make a withdrawal from that same friendship when your friend, an expert crafter, helps you make homemade party favors for your cousin's birthday party. Or, the withdrawal may happen when your friend treats you to your favorite drink during your weekly happy hour. In these examples, there's an even giving and receiving, whether through friendly advice, assistance, or an act of kindness.

While a deposit might be made as a result of a withdrawal or vice versa, it's important to treat these actions as independent "relationship transactions." You should make a deposit, not because you hope to earn a pat on the back or want something in return, but because you want to nurture a relationship and want to give your attention to someone who matters to you. Likewise, you should make a withdrawal not because you want to take advantage of someone, but because that someone is offering love, support, or knowledge to help you.

Different Types of Deposits and Withdrawals

This principle of relationship accounting can apply to anything in which you invest time and energy. Let's look at the different types of deposits and withdrawals we can make in other areas of your life:

- **YOUR THINGS:** The material items around you need deposits of your energy, time, and resources to function and stay well maintained. In a home, making deposits might involve keeping it clean, maintaining the furnace and water systems, and doing repairs when needed. For a car, making a deposit would include spending money and time to put gas in the tank, getting an engine tune-up, and keeping the tires inflated properly. Making a withdrawal would include driving the car to work every day or taking it on a long vacation. For a computer, deposits include updating the software and deleting unnecessary files, while withdrawals would be creating presentations, downloading songs, or watching movies.

- **YOUR HEALTH:** Deposits to your health include eating well, sleeping well, getting exercise, and stretching. Withdrawals might include working late or overindulging in alcohol. Tracking your health-related deposits and withdrawals is essential to your well-being, especially if you want your body to perform for you in the long-term. That is, you cannot make demands of your body if you haven't taken care of it. This is especially true as we age. If we've made too many withdrawals from our bodies in our twenties and thirties, we may not be in optimal health when we enter our forties and fifties.

- **YOUR SOCIAL COMMITMENTS:** The activities that fill your schedule, such as your job, club meetings, sports team practices, and hangouts with your social circle, usually require a deposit of your time, your participation in, and in some cases money. It's possible to deposit too much into your various social commitments or for your commitments to ask you to withdraw too much. For example, suppose you're part of a volunteer organization and you donate a large chunk of your free time organizing and planning events but don't get much support for your efforts. If you feel stressed and tired instead of excited and energized, perhaps it's time to pare back your responsibilities in this organization until the work that you're doing feels fulfilling again.

- **YOUR INFORMATION:** Choosing how to share and how to react to information with others is an exercise in making deposits and withdrawals. For example, if you choose to share a personal story about love or loss with someone, you're depositing that information. Conversely, if someone shares a personal experience with you, particularly to help you in some way, then you are making a withdrawal. When making deposits, how you share your experience makes a difference. Be mindful to avoid venting or dumping your problems on someone else; consider how the information you share about how you got through some bad situation could help or inspire the person. For example, when you're telling a friend about a bad relationship, describing how your partner betrayed you but you fell in love again. This can be a deposit to illustrate how it's possible to get to the other side of a bad breakup.

Check Your Balances

Ideally, the love, help, and guidance you put into a relationship, whether it's with your best friend or a colleague, should be approximately equal to the love, emotion, help, and guidance you receive from that person. This doesn't mean every relationship has to be equal all the time. Nobody's perfect. Sometimes our parents frustrate us, our siblings annoy us, and our friends disappoint us. Nevertheless, strive to balance your withdrawals and deposits. When your deposits are in line with your withdrawals, you'll feel more at ease. The more balanced your relationships, the more enjoyable and harmonious they will be.

As discussed in chapter 6, the best way to know where you stand with everyone in your life is to collect some data. Keeping tabs on your deposits and withdrawals will allow you to see where your energy is going. Your Relationship Ledger can help you identify the relationships that might be draining your energy or are otherwise lopsided. When you track the effort you put in versus the effort you receive, the relationships out of balance will be obvious. You might need to recalibrate your efforts or reserve your energy. For example, if a family member calls you only when they need money, a ride, or a hand with something around the house, you may not at first realize the imbalance until you sit down and analyze your deposits and withdrawals.

You might even discover that tracking your relationship transactions makes you more aware of your wonderful qualities, talents, and contributions to the world. When you're taking care of the people you love, you might not recognize how much you do every day. Recording your deposits and withdrawals will keep you from losing sight of all the important things you do for others. With this awareness, you can decide how to show up for others, making sure you do it in a way that sustains you.

Assessing your Relationship Ledger will also help you set realistic expectations of what you can give others and what others can give you. In short, you want to be giving as much as you're receiving. And while it's important to note when a friend or family member might be taking more than they give in return, you want to be most aware of your own actions and feelings. Are you the one making more deposits than withdrawals?

For example, one of my sisters gives the best advice. I'd call her any time of day, every day, if I could because she is just that good.

But before I call her now, I ask myself, "Have I deposited into this relationship recently? And how much?" And if I am feeling like I am constantly making withdrawals, I bring it up with her. If I am, she'll acknowledge it, and if not, she'll make that clear, too.

If you have a similar relationship with someone, think about whether you are always using this person to dump your drama. Instead, can you quickly bring to mind something you've done for this person? If you can't, be conscious of monopolizing your conversations with your own problems. Ask about the balance of deposits and withdrawals. Of course, this exposes your vulnerability and the potential for criticism, but it is vital for maintaining a very healthy and balanced relationship.

Safe Deposits

When it comes to friendships and business relationships, I used to be a "trust, then verify" person. I assumed people had as good intentions as I did. If I asked friends for something, I would then write thank-you notes and be prepared with a word of gratitude at every turn. I assumed when I shared my time, contacts, or advice, they would be as gracious as I was. I thought that when mistakes were made, I should quickly forgive and then get back to business as usual. But by staying in these unbalanced relationships, I was creating chaos in my life and allowing people access to me that they didn't deserve.

I had a really tough time when I decided to end a friendship because the person had betrayed me in a devastating way. I picked up a few books on having hard conversations and found one idea that instantly freed me: just because you forgive someone, that doesn't mean you should trust them or give them that access again. The book explained that access should be granted again only after they've proved they know how to treat you.

You should not trust everyone to treat you in the same manner as you treat them. But this doesn't mean people have bad intentions or that every relationship has the potential to turn toxic. Sometimes the people we love just aren't living by the principles we find important. For instance, maybe they have deep trauma they are trying to work through and the dynamics of your relationship trigger them.

I am committed to always being my authentic self. And to do that, I have to reserve part of me just for me. You need to do the same. I have learned to enjoy open, authentic relationships that are not transparent. My transparency is reserved for very few people in my life. Similarly, you can be authentic without being transparent, and you should be. The people with whom you are transparent should feel honored to know you—should cover you, pray for you, and always keep your secrets.

Always Start with Deposits

When it comes to romance, people often outline what they're looking for in a mate: the person should be funny, kind, smart, athletic, have a good job, and want children. But do we think as deeply about what we can give a mate? Consider your close friends and why they are your friends. For example, one might be super funny; another might be good for a laugh when you're feeling down or have had a bad day at work. But what do you give your friends? Do you provide the same comfort?

Because our deposits help us connect with other people, making a deposit before a withdrawal lays the foundation for a balanced relationship. That is, extending care or kindness to other people usually encourages them to do the same for you. It also helps you set the tone for a relationship—if you start a connection with someone in an act of kindness, that kind vibe will likely be an underlying current of your bond. Making a deposit can also help recalibrate a relationship that may have gone awry—say, you're feeling that a friend has become distant or you've been making a few too many withdrawals from someone lately. Making a deposit—giving your time or attention in some way or another—can show your appreciation for the friend and you will possibly reconnect.

Practice making deposits following these guidelines:

- **NOTICE WHAT SOMEONE MIGHT NEED:** Deposits require paying attention to other people and seeing if there is a way to help. I have a friend who does this so well. He is a tech genius, and he always seems to notice when I need a small tech upgrade, like the right USB cord or the right phone holder for my car; he offers just the right solution to a problem I didn't even know I had! I feel loved whenever this happens.

- **ASK YOURSELF, WHAT CAN I DO TO HELP?** Everyone has a unique talent, skill, and piece of knowledge that can be just the thing that some other person, or a group of people, needs. When you're making new connections, or nurturing a relationship that you feel needs more attention, take the time to ask yourself how you can contribute to the situation. What are you uniquely qualified to offer? This approach works especially well in group settings, where several people are coming together with a common interest—think social clubs, parent groups, and nonprofit organizations.

- **LISTEN MORE THAN YOU TALK:** People frequently ask me if I'm "still there" on phone calls because I let the person on the line speak freely, without interrupting. Yes, I am! We often listen to find a place to interject rather than listen to fully comprehend the conversation. Listening to someone else seems like such a small thing, but it has a huge impact. Similarly, meeting new people and seeking their time and expertise means nothing if you are not taking in what they are all sharing. Plus, letting people know they have been heard will strengthen your social connections. The next time someone comes to you with a problem, listen carefully. Once the person has aired their thoughts, ask if they are open to hearing your advice. If you're on a phone call, try staying quiet for a few beats longer than usual and see what results from that short silence.

- **DO A FAVOR WITHOUT EXPECTING ANYTHING IN RETURN:** Each deposit should come from a place of good intention. You've probably chosen to enter into a relationship with your people or signed up for an activity because it feels like a good idea to do so. The effort you put into maintaining those relationships and participating in that activity should also feel good. Giving support or spending time with something because you *care* will definitely be more rewarding than making an effort simply because you want something in return. For example, suppose you stop by the drugstore on a quick errand before meeting your sister for a movie. At the store, you notice your sister's favorite candy on sale. You might surprise her with the candy, just because you want her to enjoy her favorite snack during the movie.

- **MAKING A DEPOSIT CAN BE EASIER THAN YOU THINK:** Sometimes doing a low-lift favor for someone can provide a high-worth deposit into the relationship bank. Take, for example, doing a favor for a fellow mom. You pick up your child's friend from school and drop them off at home. For you, it was a low lift—the child's home is on the way to yours and it took hardly any extra time to head there. For that child's mom, though, you might have made her afternoon. She may have needed that time to do something else, and she's happy to see her child spend some extra time with your kid after school. The mom will likely feel twice as good receiving the favor than the effort it took you to provide it.

- **SHOW CARE AND GRATITUDE:** Deposits can be seen as an act of care. Something as simple as showing up for an activity or a previous commitment, giving words of encouragement to someone who's about to make a big move, or even saying thank-you to someone for something they've done—all these count as small deposits. And small moments of gratitude often make big impressions on other people, so don't discount them.

When Is a Deposit *Really* a Deposit?

Making a deposit can feel great, but if it leaves you feeling depleted and disappointed, it may not actually be a deposit. There are times when a deposit is a withdrawal in disguise. This often happens because you are either expecting something in return—and are disappointed if you don't receive it—or feeling less than content after giving your time and attention to someone else.

To help determine whether a deposit is really a deposit, use the examples in the table on page 141 to see if you fall into common "deposit traps." Remember, a deposit should feel good to give. It shouldn't require you to set aside your needs and it shouldn't come with strings attached.

DEPOSIT	WITHDRAWAL
You've done a favor for a friend without expecting anything in return.	You've done a favor for a friend, expecting they'll do one for you in return.
You loaned a family member money.	You loaned a family member money, expecting they'll pay you back with interest or buy you something in return.
You provided a reference for someone for a job or loan.	You provided a reference for someone for a job or loan, but are disappointed when the person doesn't offer you one in return.
You lent a friend an expensive dress for an event.	You lent a friend an expensive dress for an event but feel bummed out when the friend offers you a less expensive dress to borrow another day.
You offer to water your aunt's houseplants while she is on vacation.	You offered to water your aunt's houseplants even though her house is a long drive away and you were hoping to save gas money this month.

instant elevation with . . .

SUSAN MCPHERSON

Susan McPherson is a serial connector, angel investor, and corporate responsibility expert. She is the founder and CEO of McPherson Strategies, and the author of The Lost Art of Connecting, *a guide to building and prioritizing meaningful connections. Here, she shares another perspective on being of service to others.*

Happiness and meaningful connections are intertwined. If we look back at the lives we have lived to date, I bet you would agree with me that almost every momentous happening you've experienced occurred because of your connections. New experiences, untapped causes, job opportunities, romantic partners—all these things came from others we've connected with.

In my book, I explain my Gather, Ask, Do method, a series of steps for building meaningful connections and prioritizing them in your life. The key idea in this methodology is to lead with how you can be helpful to others. This is the antithesis of what we are taught when we learned to network. Then, we learned to walk into rooms with the goal of leaving with new contacts who could provide us help. Believe me, when you flip that switch and show others how you can support them, the help will be returned in spades. When you learn to ask meaningful questions about others' hopes and dreams, and listen carefully to their answers, you show them you have a unique gift: the ability to be of service to others.

Before you think that you have no time to help others, I beg to differ. This is a methodology you can practice over a lifetime. And it could be as simple as making an introduction for someone, recommending a new podcast or newsletter, or showcasing someone's accomplishments on social media.

Exercise: Create a Relationship Ledger

Working toward your goal will require you to make many different types of deposits and withdrawals. In this exercise, you record the resources you've received and given to others using a Relationship Ledger (see also page 144). You can use this ledger to track all the transactions related to one relationship or keep tabs on all your relationships over a set period of time. Taking stock of where your time and energy is going will help you determine if you're giving too much or too little, and it will show you which relationships could use more deposits.

For each recipient, write down the event or time frame of the transaction and a description of the deposit and/or withdrawal. Use the "How Do I Feel?" column to note your feelings concerning the transaction afterward.

Here are some sample entries to help you get started:

RECIPIENT	EVENT	DEPOSIT	WITHDRAWAL	HOW DO I FEEL?
Best friend	Met for coffee	Gave advice on her career move	Discussed my own frustrations at work	I am so glad to feel seen by her and do the same in return.
Sister	Phone call	Spent an hour listening to her complain about our brother not including her in his holiday dinner	None	I feel emotionally drained from listening, and from playing mediator between two siblings.

RECIPIENT	EVENT	DEPOSIT	WITHDRAWAL	HOW DO I FEEL?

Exercise: Plan Your Next Deposits

You may have already identified some relationships in your life that need some improvement. If so, here's a great opportunity to make some small deposits toward balancing your ledger. Making deposits of good or kindness toward someone (or something) might revitalize a relationship that may have fizzled, and it will help you reconnect on better terms.

Using the prompts on this page, list five ideas for deposits. You can gift your time, energy, and knowledge. Be creative! If you get stuck, use the deposits you recorded in your Relationship Ledger (see page 143).

1. Description of deposit: _____
Scheduled for: _____
Pay to:_____

2. Description of deposit: _____
Scheduled for: _____
Pay to:_____

3. Description of deposit: _____
Scheduled for: _____
Pay to:_____

4. Description of deposit: _____
Scheduled for: _____
Pay to:_____

5. Description of deposit: _____
Scheduled for: _____
Pay to:_____

PHASE THREE

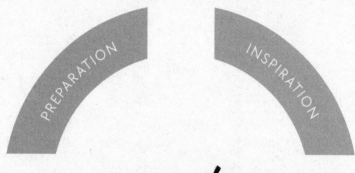

PREPARATION

INSPIRATION

recreation

TRANSFORMATION

RECREATION

CHAPTER 11

Get Ready to Recreate!

Ten years after I founded my agency, I won what I thought was the golden ticket: a Fortune 500, seven-figure client. This was what I'd worked for my entire career. After we finalized the paperwork, I was elated that things were finally falling into place. But behind the scenes, I was quietly falling apart.

After years of creating and launching project after project, I wasn't just tired and overwhelmed. My health was also suffering. My hair was beginning to fall out. I developed an ulcer, and I started having stomach pains from the constant anxiety. Eventually the marketing products I was launching weren't as good as they could have been. During a big session at work, I felt like I was crawling to the finish line.

I knew I worked hard, but I didn't know why I was so burnt out. I thought I was getting the hang of taking time for myself. I'd started going on girls' trips and group vacations, exercising regularly, and eating really healthy foods. I would return from traveling or a hangout with friends feeling a little better, but the stress returned soon after.

After coming home from an especially exhausting work trip, I spent time with my niece, Phoebe, who was a toddler at the time. I loved how she played. She always found a way to get all her aunts involved in art projects, cooking, and her favorite TV shows. We were fully immersed with her, and I would leave those times together feeling refreshed. The new ideas I'd struggled to think through otherwise came easily after those playdates with Phoebe. Now, I was starting to put the pieces of the puzzle together.

I realized I wasn't using my trips, exercise, or breaks from work as opportunities to reset my thinking and recharge my batteries. Often, I was still thinking about work when I was supposed to be taking a break. I wasn't fully present for the fun activities; my thoughts kept drifting toward my next deadline, a project that needed my input, or an email that called for a response. So, I started scheduling proper downtime. I took the time to simply pause between projects—no laptop time, no meetings, and very few phone calls. Giving my brain some uninterrupted time to rest eventually helped me feel more in control, less scattered, and less stressed.

In the Preparation and Inspiration phases, you might have been in the weeds with working toward your goal—making the rituals, collecting the data, planning the actions, doing what you needed to get there. Now that you're geared up and ready to go, it's time to pause! The Recreation phase is your chance to set aside time for rest and play, which will ensure you don't end up like pre–Elevation Approach me—completely toasted.

What Recreation Is

Let's take a look at what recreation means for you at this point of the Elevation Approach:

UNSTRUCTURED: Recreation serves as a counterpoint to the structured duties of your everyday life. It has as few rules and time constraints as possible to allow for unrestricted play and discovery.

ENJOYABLE: Recreation includes activities that make you feel good or that you enjoy doing.

TIME TO RECOVER: Recreation refreshes your mind and body. Just as the body needs rest after a workout, the mind needs time to recover from problem-solving and other daily work.

REFRESHING: Recreation allows you to hit the pause button on the business of life and to take a breather. Whether you choose to do something different, go somewhere else, or do absolutely nothing, this time allows you to step away from thinking about your regular responsibilities.

What Recreation Is NOT

To be effective, your recreation should avoid the following pitfalls:

FORCED: Recreation should not feel like another obligation or task. Recreation should feel natural and involve pursuits you are excited to do.

WORK: Recreation should feel like a respite from work, with its own routine, rhythm, and activity. However you decide to take a break, you need to adopt a gentler pace and feel at ease and relaxed.

DANGEROUS: While getting out of your safe zone is discussed in the next chapter, your chosen recreation should not be risky to you. Avoid any activities that put your life in danger or your health at risk.

Reset with Rest

Many places around the world prioritize rest for people. In Spain, Greece, and many other countries, the siesta is observed. Businesses and schools close in the afternoon, so people can head home for an extended lunch with family and an afternoon rest. Workers in European countries often also have long summer and winter holidays; many take off the entire month of August for a summer break and three weeks in December for the winter holidays. Try sending an email to a European client in August; I guarantee you will not get a response until after Labor Day.

For many of us, especially in the United States, where workplaces don't encourage employees to take time off and working overtime can earn you a badge of honor, making time for rest can seem counterproductive. But skipping these breaks prevents us from bringing our projects to fruition and executing our ideas. We get stuck on a hamster wheel of productivity, but the wheel can go only so fast and spin so long before it breaks. Rest lets us step off the wheel before it's too late.

Rest also allows creativity to thrive by giving your mind the space to just think and observe. It helps you reset after all the work you've done in the first two phases. Whereas Preparation and Inspiration were about gathering your tools and taking in information from the world around you, Recreation is the time to decompress and allow what you've learned to settle in.

When you pull your nose off the grindstone and look around, you begin to make unexpected connections that can lead to new ideas. You are open to an approach or method radically different from what you've been doing. Putting some distance between you and your work ultimately helps you filter out ideas that don't work or notice if something about your process isn't working as well as expected. Sometimes, the only way to truly understand and clearly observe something, even if it's just the air moving in and out of your lungs, is to step away from it.

This unstructured, behind-the-scenes processing is one of my favorite parts of Recreation. When I'm relaxed and well rested, the ideas seem to magically come my way. I find solutions to business problems. When I return to my work, I can stay focused longer and have more energy for brainstorming. It sometimes even feels like I'm hardly working at all.

The Power of Play

When I was struggling with burnout, learning how to take a break was only half the battle. I also had to figure out how to recreate. Spending time with the children in my life helped me make an important discovery: what I was missing from my life was time to play. I hadn't given myself enough opportunities to explore my creativity and just have fun.

Play is an essential component of recreation. It fires up your curiosity. It allows your mind to wander and explore new fields. It allows you to indulge in your creativity and try hobbies, sports, or activities outside of work, thereby relieving stress and eventually leading you to the things that spark pure, unadulterated joy.

Play also allows you to drop any expectations you have of yourself and of the world around you; you can just indulge in an activity for the sake of it. You don't have to be good or bad or produce something profound. You can simply be in the moment, enjoying what's in front of you, basking in that feeling for as long as you want.

Additionally, play helps you achieve more at work. Yes, the point of play is to enjoy life outside of work, but you won't derail your progress just because you take a pause for fun. In fact, the results from your recess will help you achieve more in the long term.

During the pandemic lockdown, many people had more time at home to indulge in play and to attend to their hobbies. People baked sourdough bread in between their video calls, learned how to play an instrument, or picked up the instruments they practiced as children. Some people wrote screenplays or took up gardening, growing herbs on their kitchen windowsills. For me, I played with food. I became a vegan for eight weeks and learned about the plant-based meals and diet plans. I found new recipes and tried out new food combinations and textures. "Playing" with my food introduced a spark of novelty to my day, even if I had to spend that day indoors—and it provided comfort during a stressful time. For many, those experiments with new skills, crafts, or activities created joy and were happy diversions from the heavier circumstances of the time. Play provides levity and delight for all our days, helping us realign our lives with actions that truly light up our souls.

Exercise: Create a Recreation Playbook

Play is an important component of the Recreation phase, but adults often don't make enough time for it. In this exercise, you create a Recreation Playbook, using the table on page 155 to list your favorite games, people, places, and so forth, and end up with a catalog of activities.

After completing this exercise, you can refer to this catalog the next time you're in need of play. Schedule some time to partake in these activities regularly. Even a few minutes here or there is enough to bring a smile to your face.

Types of Recreation

There are many forms of recreation. I've listed four different types of recreation, based on duration.

BREAK: I think of a break as a short pause or recess from your work. A break can be as short as a few minutes or can last a day or two. I like doing something mindless on my breaks, like watching television or getting a manicure. Sometimes, I do nothing and let myself just be in the moment.

YOUR PERSONAL PLAYBOOK

Favorite Activities	
Favorite People	
Favorite Places	
Favorite Sports	
Favorite Hobbies	
Favorite Games	

PLAY: Play often involves a short structured or unstructured activity. Think sports games, an art class, a bike ride, or an hour spent sewing or knitting. But play can also be as simple as playing on a swing at the playground with your kids or experimenting with new makeup.

VACATION: A vacation stands out from the first two types of recreation as it involves a longer break from your work, making it easier to completely disconnect from it all. You might spend a few days, maybe a week or two, relaxing in a leisure spot.

SABBATICAL: A sabbatical is an extended period of time away from work. When people opt for a sabbatical, they may leave their job for months or even years at a time. Sabbaticals present the opportunity to try out a lifestyle change or embark on a long-term adventure, whether it's traveling around the world, living on a boat, or going off the grid. Because of their length, sabbaticals involve a considerable amount of time away from any ideas or tasks related to your goal as well.

———————

Depending on what you've been doing in the Preparation and Inspiration phases, you might be ready for a long vacation so as to reset and regroup, or just need a short break to relax your mind. You might start with one long recess from work, or consider scheduling several shorter, recurring breaks as you continue working toward your goal. Either option is fine, as long as your Recreation experience is unstructured and joyful.

Recreate Right

Picture this scene: You're spending a leisurely morning at your local park. You want to take a moment to view the beautiful scenery and enjoy the fresh air. You think, *Great, I'm going to sit down. While I'm at this bench, why don't I take a quick look at my emails?*

You may have thought you were taking a break when you walked out the door, but this visit to the park isn't true recreation. You were just changing your work venue from desk to park.

To make sure you're getting the true break you deserve, here's a quick set of questions to help you determine if you are on a break. If you answer no to any of these five questions, consider a different activity or don't make any plans or activities at all.

1. Are you in a different place from where you usually work on your project? YES NO
2. Are you away from your work supplies and communication (emails, spreadsheets, props, tools, etc.)? YES NO
3. Are you doing something that makes you forget about any challenges you have on your project? YES NO
4. Are you relaxed? YES NO
5. Are you doing something that does not have a goal or purpose other than enjoyment and fun? YES NO

Troubleshooting: "Help, I'm Stuck!"

You've opted to take some well-earned time, and now you feel like you're on a permanent vacation. You're beginning to worry that you're having too much fun to return to your goal. You start wondering if you're getting sidetracked.

Remember that the goal of the Elevation Approach is to help you find harmony in your work and play. Here are a few ways to make sure your time in Recreation doesn't lead you too far from your goal:

- **SET A TIME LIMIT:** Decide the duration of your break before you start. How long do you need? A day? A week? A month? It's okay to put aside your goal for an extended time, as long as you can commit to returning to it when your rest has ended.

- **HAVE A PLANNED REENTRY ACTIVITY:** If you find your break becoming too unfocused and open-ended, choose a task or establish a routine that will gently help you get back to work. For example, if you've put down a writing project, use the Recreation phase to do an activity that is unrelated to your project but that draws upon the same skills. For instance, a crossword puzzle with your morning coffee is a great play activity because it is a fun and relaxing game using your writing and language skills. Once you've completed your recreational activity, turn your attention back to your project.

- **HANG OUT WITH A BREAK BUDDY:** A break buddy is a person you equate with fun and consider a great go-to source for recreation. If you tend to spend too much time recreating, or have taken too long a break, scheduling your recreation sessions in line with a break buddy's availability can keep your breaks from stretching on endlessly. For example, my time with my niece is pure, unadulterated fun. I know I will have a proper reprieve from work when I hang out with her, and I know that after our playdate is over, it's time to get back to the task at hand.

- **JOURNAL DURING YOUR BREAK:** Journaling will encourage you to make notes of any ideas, solutions, feelings, or thoughts you have during Recreation. Oftentimes people take a break from their goals because they're feeling exasperated, tired, frustrated, or hopeless, and their goal seems far away. But writing down your thoughts and recording the things you've done so far allows you to see how far you've come and will motivate you to keep going.

I'm Ready. Now What?

If you're in the Recreation phase of the Elevation Approach, congratulations! You've likely prepared, planned, and made some moves toward bringing more harmony to your life. The three principles of the Recreation phase are about taking a break from this work and giving yourself a chance to process and refocus.

First, we will show you how to **get outside of your safe zone**. Whether it's taking the long walk to work or visiting a new restaurant, now is the time to give something new a try. Not only does it keep you sharp mentally and physically, but it also allows you to explore ideas and opportunities you haven't before had the chance to consider.

Next, you will **move**. Walk, dance, run, or jump! This principle is about leisurely movement that gets you out of your usual grind.

Finally, you will learn how to **create joy.** There's a difference between joy and happiness, and understanding this distinction will help you build a lifetime of joy rather than pursue a passing moment of happiness. You'll learn how to define what brings you joy and how best to attract those things into your life every day.

THREE QUESTIONS FOR RECREATION

When you've worked through these three principles of Recreation, you will be well prepared to begin the last phase of the Elevation

Approach. You'll know you're ready for Transformation when you can answer yes to these three questions:

1. Have I gotten out of my normal routine and tried something new?
2. Have I practiced some form of movement that has no other purpose than to make me feel good?
3. Have I pinpointed the sources of joy in my life?

CHAPTER 12

Principle #7: Get Outside of Your Safe Zone

My safe zones embody what I expect from my environment. When I wake up in the morning in my own home, I know what I'll eat, where things are, how long it will take me to get to the office. At work, my safe zone is taking on the same type of projects as I have before. Outside of work, it's going to the same place on vacation. It's even going to the same coffee shop because they know how to make my cappuccino with almond milk without overfrothing it. That is, your safe zone is what you know. It's the same route to the grocery store, the same workout, the same take-out meals, the same clothes, and the same friends who play the same card games every weekend. It's where you know nothing bad will happen. It's what is predictable, familiar, and comforting.

While consistency is a great thing to have during times of stress, too much consistency can leave a person a bit dull, mentally and emotionally. It certainly makes me feel bored. I start making decisions on autopilot, without considering unique circumstances or whether my needs have changed. Eventually, the things around me lose their sparkle, even the things I have always loved.

Getting out of your safe zone means doing something that takes you out of your normal routines so you can regain that sparkle. While leaving your safe zone doesn't always involve travel or any sort of physical displacement, you might find yourself going to places that you wouldn't have expected to. And while you certainly don't have to seek danger, you might feel a bit nervous or anxious, maybe even scared.

If you want to reach a goal or bring work-life harmony into your life, you need to try something new. Recreation is the ideal time to leave your safe zone. Stepping into the unknown or unfamiliar will allow you to ponder new ideas. During the Preparation and Inspiration phases, you did a lot of work toward your goal without taking a break to gain some perspective. Now, getting out of your safe zone can remove you from your work and day-to-day environment, helping you think beyond what you know and consider new possibilities.

Recreation itself may be something outside your safe zone if you rarely take a break from work. Blame guilt or a lack of time, but perhaps you've found it easier, or more familiar or comfortable, to keep working. Perhaps you're nervous that taking a break will derail your progress. Don't worry, with the Elevation Approach, getting out of your safe zone isn't about losing momentum. It's about gaining a chance to see potential, to improve upon what you're doing. You can only see that potential when you step away from the routine. And that potential, that new perspective, is not possible without taking the pause, without stepping out of your safe zone and exposing yourself to something new.

Let's dive deeper into how looking beyond the familiar can move you along the Elevation Approach.

A Path to Self-Discovery

In my early thirties, I went through a devastating breakup. I was dating a wonderful guy who was creative, kind, supportive, and funny. We were together for more than a year, but we parted ways because we wanted different things in life. I lost not only my boyfriend but also my best friend.

With past breakups, I usually blamed the guy for not living up to my expectations or for doing something I didn't like—two things that served as red flags in a relationship. This breakup, though, had taken me out of my safe zone, leaving me clueless. My ex was a great guy, we got along well, and we were happy together, but somehow it just didn't work.

As part of my healing process, I decided to take up yoga. I had tried a few classes before, but I was no yogi and I certainly couldn't tell you what an *adho mukha svanasana* was (that's downward dog, in Sanskrit). I went to my first class feeling intimidated, with low expectations.

Many people seek out yoga because they are looking for balance and calm. I chose yoga because I didn't know how to do it—and I didn't *have* to know how to do it. Like many women, I felt like I was supposed to have my life figured out by now. I was supposed to have all the answers because people relied on me. Because I was successful in other areas of my life, I felt pressure to be successful in all areas of my life. These are hardly fair assumptions—women, myself included, are allowed to not know everything all the time.

The beauty of yoga is that you can walk into any class knowing nothing at all. At my first class, I listened to the instructor walk everyone, including the more advanced students, through each pose. I noticed how she always gave us the *option* to do each one. It didn't matter if I could do a headstand or just sat on my mat and breathed deeply. It didn't even matter if I cried in class, because everyone was sweaty and needed to wipe their faces the entire time. As long as I was trying my best, I was doing yoga.

At the end of my first class, I felt at ease. I was relaxed from the actual practice, but also was calm after realizing I could get through something I had no idea how to do—in my own way, on my own time, with no judgment. That is, yoga gave me permission to not have all the answers. It helped me realize I would be okay if I couldn't find solutions to every problem or give immediate answers to all the questions in my life. Each class helped me become more comfortable with uncertainty and to understand that eventually I would regain my footing. I even fell in love again . . . with yoga. It's become one of the most healing practices I've ever introduced into my life.

Getting out of your safe zone forces your brain to work in ways it's not used to. While exposing yourself to a new way of thinking may be uncomfortable, it might help you rethink solutions to problems and learn how to handle adversity. Dealing with the unfamiliar, or the unpredictable, forces us to get familiar with the uncomfortable. It's an exercise that builds resilience and confidence in our own strengths. If we can sit in uncomfortable situations—say, a challenging yoga pose—we eventually realize that the pose won't break us, and that the longer we sit in the discomfort, the less discomforting it is. Muscles stretch, and as we learn how our bodies react to certain poses, so does our trust in our ability to reach our best potential.

Now imagine if you practice that same skill to sit with the

discomfort of, say, financial trouble. Instead of running from the discomfort, you could pause long enough to find a solution to the problem. You might come to terms with how much you owe to others and develop a plan for paying off creditors or filing for bankruptcy. And the longer you sit in the reality of the situation and research the solutions, the more confident you'll be with the next right move. You might also realize that the challenge will not destroy you but, rather, strengthen that muscle of resilience in you for future challenges. Every time you step out of your safe zone, you strengthen your ability to face the unknowns in life.

Have Fun Without Judgment

Another benefit of getting out of your safe zone is the chance to try something new or take a risk, with little judgment or expectation. For example, I recently signed up for a wine tour around France with my friend's wine club. I was worried about joining a tour with people who would most likely be more knowledgeable about wine. But I joined anyway because I wanted to learn more about enjoying wine. It was also a great excuse to participate in an activity completely unrelated to my work. There would be no networking, no brand building, and nobody I needed to impress. It would be just me and other people who liked wine.

Though I was nervous at the start, the wine tour ultimately broadened my horizons. It was fun to learn something new about that wide world of wine, especially from my new friends. While I was familiar with the types of wine I liked—mostly those from New Zealand or Australia—the tour expanded my palate, gave me the amazing opportunity to visit vineyards, presented inspiring female winemakers, and connected me with new friends, all while exploring France.

Sometimes we're afraid to get out and try something unfamiliar because we put too much stock in what other people think of us. We might feel guilty about enjoying something others may find strange or at least out of the ordinary. But getting out of your safe zone is essential to personal growth. When you do things that are unfamiliar, you have a chance to experiment and learn what happens when you approach something one step at a time. Plus, you usually aren't expected to master an activity in one take. You'll be surprised at how much more you can learn, even about subjects you think you already know plenty about. That feeling of growth and progression is what feeds our souls and elevates our lives to their highest potential.

Taking Your Brain Out of Your Safe Zone

Thanks to the concept of neuroplasticity, getting out of your safe zone can be good for your brain. Neuroplasticity is the brain's ability to adapt to new experiences. There are two main types of neuroplasticity: functional plasticity, in which the brain moves a function from a damaged area to an undamaged area, and structural plasticity, in which the brain changes its physical structure by learning. The more plasticity our brains have, the smarter and more efficient we are in adapting to changes in our environment, whether those changes come from learning a new sport, reading a new book, or recovering from a brain injury.

Why is this important? Humans are born with about 2,500 synapses, or small gaps between the neurons that relay nerve impulses. These impulses, or messages, tell our brains how to operate our body and respond to our environment—for example, how to walk, talk, eat, and process information.

By the age of three, we have about 15,000 of these synapses per neuron, as our little bodies are growing so rapidly and quickly taking in information about their world in order to function. As we grow, the synapses that get used the most frequently become stronger, while the ones we don't use get weaker and eventually shut down. This process is known as synaptic pruning. By the time we're adults, we have only half the synapses we did as a toddler.

As we age, we have fewer synapses to help us adjust to changes in the brain. The good news is that we increase the brain's neuroplasticity by taking on new tasks and activities that stimulate new or weaker brain synapses. These tasks, such as learning a new language, taking up a new sport, learning a new instrument, traveling, and reading, aren't just fun—they're also good for your brain!

Get Up and Get Out of Your Safe Zone

You don't have to go through a big life change or drastically disrupt your daily rhythm to practice this principle. Getting out of your safe zone can be as simple as going to a new neighborhood for dinner, trying a new hairstyle or hair color, or reading a book from a different genre. During your daily routine. There are easy, quick, and practical ideas to get out of your safe zone every day:

- **PLAN A SOLO ACTIVITY:** Go on an outing by yourself—no friends, no children, and if you can, no phone or computer. For example, try eating at a restaurant or going to a concert by yourself.
- **TRAVEL:** If you can travel, do it frequently. You will discover new things about yourself and expose yourself to different traditions and customs. You don't have to go far to see new sights. Taking a drive an hour outside of town or spending an afternoon in a new neighborhood might broaden your horizons.
- **DO THE OPPOSITE OF WHAT YOU NORMALLY DO:** Try drinking tea instead of coffee one morning. Instead of taking the train, try biking to work. Here's a super-easy idea: try using

your nondominant hand to write or do activities. That small change will at least make you feel grateful for your dominant hand.

- **GIVE UP A HABIT OR A ROUTINE:** Try taking something out of your usual routine for a day or two and see how it affects your life. This will force you to try alternative means to complete tasks and consider other solutions. For example, if you give up social media for a day, or stop using your phone, how will you spend the time you normally use for your apps? What other ways can you use to communicate with people?

- **RETREAT:** Do you find yourself working all the time? Are you always doing a project, cleaning the house, or taking care of something? Maybe doing absolutely nothing is a way to get out of your safe zone, especially if you're used to being busy.

Get Out There!

- Sign up for a new exercise class.
- Try a new coffee shop or restaurant.
- Try a new cuisine or type of food.
- Cook a meal for yourself, or someone else, one you've never made before.
- Go to a museum.
- Check out a new neighborhood in your area. Visit local attractions and stop by the local hangouts.
- Read a book in a genre you haven't tried before.
- Grab a coffee with a casual acquaintance whom you don't know well.
- Change your commute. Take an earlier train or a different route. Or walk!
- Add your own idea:_____

instant elevation with . . .

CINDY KENT

A longtime executive in the medical industry, Cindy Kent is the chief operating officer of the healthcare start-up Everly Health. She's had several big life events that have taken her far out of her comfort zone in the past five years. Here, she shares what she learned:

I found myself "most" outside my safe zone in 2018. I had been working in healthcare for over twenty-five years and had been with my latest company for nearly five years. While working with the executive team on my next project, most likely an international move, I realized what I wanted most was a break—for both personal and professional reasons. That summer, I started working on a plan for what I thought would be a six-month sabbatical. I consulted with friends and mentors, and the overwhelming majority was skeptical about my resigning from a role without having another job lined up. In June, after much introspection and prayer, I decided to leave my job as president of Infection Prevention at 3M—the iconic Post-It note maker. I was the sole financial provider for my household, so this big decision impacted not only me but also my family.

What I didn't anticipate was that just four months later, I would move out of our home and begin divorce proceedings after nearly fifteen years of marriage. Talk about a double whammy! It was a lot to process all at once. And because I was the breadwinner, I had to split all my assets. I found myself a divorced, middle-aged woman without a job and needing to financially rebuild. I also didn't have a distraction to help absorb my attention and the emotions from my failed marriage.

One of my mentors encouraged me to pick a personal theme song that would carry me through moments of doubt or fear. My theme song was Gloria Gaynor's "I Will Survive." I played it constantly. And survived is exactly what I did.

Rather than sitting around bemoaning my loss of security and safety, I committed myself to moving forward. I went to the gym every day and began to take on more speaking engagements. I joined Best Buy's board of directors, made time to network for my next role, and traveled extensively the following year. The planned six-month sabbatical turned out to be a full eighteen months. Serendipitously, the role I accepted took me back to my hometown of Nashville, Tennessee, in January 2020—two months before the global pandemic of Covid-19. In my entire career, I had either lived or worked near my very large extended family, who were nearly all in the greater Nashville area. Now, when we needed the support of one another most, we were living in proximity of one another. And within two years I was able to double the assets I had given up in the divorce.

The last few years have taken me further outside my safe zone than I expected or anticipated. There were so many changes, and they were all at once—but I simply faced each situation as it arose and made one decision at a time. One day, I looked up and realized just how far I'd come (and grown), and how much wiser, stronger, and even happier I was; that's because each decision laid the foundation for my personal path away from safety and comfort. It took these experiences to expose my strengths. I now trust myself to bounce back from negative experiences, and my inner circle is so much tighter because I have learned whom I could rely on most. There is a maturation and perspective that only life and rebounding from failure can teach you.

Exercise: Take More Steps

Doing new things can be scary. That said, you've taken the baby steps toward getting out of your safe zone—you've picked up this book and started the Elevation Approach. And you've already done things outside your safe zone in its first few phases.

If you feel a pang of fear at the prospect of revamping your routine, this exercise will help you acknowledge the small steps you've already made outside your safe zone and will encourage you to continue moving away from your familiar routines.

1. Think back to the big goal you made at the beginning of this book. Are there things about that goal that scare you? Even the small things? Are you afraid to, say, cut back on spending money on haircuts because you fear your hair will look a hot mess?

2. Write down three routines you've followed as you completed the Preparation and Inspiration phases of the Elevation Approach. For example, perhaps you set aside an hour each evening to work on your goal, chatted about your new ideas with a friend during your weekly catch-ups, or got into the habit of eating toast for breakfast because it was quick and easy.

3. In the other space, describe how you can change your routine further. For instance, you can try setting aside one hour instead of forty-five minutes for a goal-related activity, share your ideas with a family member, or make a specific tweak in one of your goal-related strategies, for example, switching out the toast for a bowl of oatmeal if you have a healthy eating related goal.

4. For the next week, implement these three changes to your routine. At the end of each day, describe your experience. Did you enjoy trying something new, or was the change more disruptive than expected? What did you learn from the experience? Will you adjust your routine based on what happened?

CHAPTER 13

Principle #8: Move

My brother Marcus has spent the last decade living in Italy. His wife is Italian, and they have two young children. When I visit him and his family, I see many beautiful parts of the country—on foot.

I easily walk 20,000 steps per day, and every element of my life seems to involve movement. We walk to the grocery store. We walk to the bus stop and to public transportation to get to museums, or we go to the market and to restaurants, even though my brother's family has a car. After we eat a big meal, we walk some more.

When we're walking through Florence, I love seeing the people outside, living life. You see older friends hanging out together, enjoying a coffee, playing a game, or just chatting. And you see multiple generations spending time together—a grandson holding his grandmother's hand. Everybody seems present, engaged with their surroundings and with one another. No one is on the phone while trying to make their way down the sidewalk. Many people are walking for the sake of walking. They walk because there are beautiful things to see and people to talk with.

During the pandemic, my experiences in Italy inspired me to move to a town that would allow me to walk everywhere. I can now go days at a time without driving, and on most days, I try to walk at least three miles. For me, walking helps me do my best thinking. There is something about a leisurely stroll that allows me to discover new ideas, mull over the events of the day, or work around an obstacle. And it makes me feel good.

In this second principle of the Recreation phase, I ask you to make movement an essential part of your everyday life. While I couldn't imagine creating a plan for work-life harmony that didn't involve moving your body, I'm not telling you to exercise or improve your fitness. Instead, I'm encouraging you to move your body in any way you like.

What Is Movement, Really?

With this principle, *to move* means to get your body into action. Movement can take whatever form you want—walking, running, cycling, dance, hula-hooping, or double Dutch in the park. Think of movement as a physical form of play. Your body is in motion for no reason but for your pure enjoyment. There are no expectations and no rules. Whatever feels good to you, do it!

As with many aspects of the Elevation Approach, movement— what it looks like and what it entails—is customizable. Do what you can with the effort that's available to you. Don't judge yourself by anybody else's standards for movement. Movement is whatever your body enjoys doing, not what it has to do or can't do. Your movement doesn't need to match anybody else's movement.

The type of movement you practice can change, depending on how your body feels. For example, my dad's relationship with movement has changed. Before he became ill, he used to walk five miles a day. Now, he's thrilled if he can get the mail every day and just feel the sun on his face. He loves to sit outside and read or work on his crossword puzzles. He's conscious to move to different parts of the house so he doesn't sit in a same space for an entire day. He's a great example that how we move can change, especially as we age or experience a shift in our mobility.

Five Benefits of Movement

1. **MOVEMENT IS A SOURCE OF FUN AND PLAY:** From dance, to skipping, to pushing yourself across a pool on an oversized flamingo, movement is motion without rules. Don't worry about not knowing how to do something. There's no wrong way to move.

2. **MOVEMENT HELPS YOU CONNECT WITH THE OUTSIDE WORLD AND STEP OUTSIDE YOUR HEAD:** Sometimes we get caught up with our thoughts, running through the same ones over and over again. Movement can help interrupt those looping thoughts and give our minds a break, which makes it easier to pay attention to the world around us so that new thoughts and ideas can pop in.

3. **MOVEMENT HELPS US LET GO OF COMPARISON:** With movement, you have the chance to enjoy an activity that doesn't involve competing or comparing yourself to anyone else.

4. **MOVEMENT IS A SOURCE OF JOY:** Activities for movement are sources of joy. Movement involves actions your body feels good doing.

5. **MOVEMENT CAN BE A SOURCE OF CREATIVITY:** Movement allows you to express yourself with your body. Dance and

gymnastics, for example, are beautiful forms of self-expression, but so, too, are things like tai chi, stretching, or doing the limbo.

Why Not Exercise?

We already know the many of the benefits of exercise, but while exercise certainly involves movement, it's not the type of movement we want to practice with this principle of recreation.

Exercise often involves physical activity that has an end goal. You might have a fitness routine because you want to burn calories, run a certain number of miles, or learn a new skill. In fact, some of our workout routines bring out our results-driven, competitive sides. We're encouraged to set targets, check our progress, and compare our results against those of our peers.

In my case, exercise was even doing me more harm than good. When I was running Buzz Marketing Group, I squeezed in boot-camp classes and workouts with a trainer after work and between meetings. I thought my workouts were delivering a much-needed stress release. But during a massage on a work trip, I learned the opposite was true. After working with my tense muscles and noticing how I had trouble relaxing my body, my massage therapist told me that exercise had made my body accustomed to stress and recognized it as its baseline status.

If you're a person who loves an intense workout or an organized workout routine, you might not be used to moving without purpose, but you don't always need to stretch your limits, beat your best time, or cross a finish line. Your body might even thank you if you don't always move it in a particular way or with a particular goal in mind.

Get Up and Go

There are many ways you can incorporate fun, carefree, feel-good movement into your life. You want to move your body in ways that get you singing, smiling, and feeling energized. If you've always wanted to take salsa lessons or learn a new sport, now's the time. If you're stumped for some ideas about getting more movement into your days, here are some suggestions.

DANCE: Throw on some music and two-step your way across the room. Or snap your fingers and bop your head to dance.

INDULGE IN KIDS' PLAY: Kids are always moving. They run, jump, skip, hop, and dance with pure abandon and joy. After we reach a certain age, we don't partake in those activities as often as we once did. Next time you're looking for ideas for movement, try skipping, hula-hooping, or jumping rope.

USE YOUR COMMUTE AS A MOVEMENT BREAK: Use your daily travels as a way to sneak in movement. If you can, walk to work because it's a great way to get more movement; you can make it fun by listening to music or a podcast along the way. You can also look at how you travel to the grocery store, make your school pickups, or reach any other place you come to and go from regularly. How can you make your transportation more fun? Can you take a scooter or bike? Roller skates or unicycle?

FOCUS ON YOUR ENJOYMENT: If you want to move by learning a new sport or activity, that's great! There's fun in learning, but make sure you're taking up that new activity because the experience will bring you joy, not because you feel you have to do it or you're trying to accomplish or win something. When you're doing things centered on joy, you relieve your stress and give yourself a chance to relax—two objectives that lead to more harmony in your life.

ENLIST A FRIEND: If you've been dying to try a new activity or need fresh ideas for movement, ask a friend for help. Movement buddies will hold you accountable, and getting involved in a new activity is usually easier with a friend.

instant elevation with . . .

MICHELE PROMAULAYKO

Michele Promaulayko is the vice president of content for THE WELL, author of Sugar-Free 3, and cohost of the podcast Messy Situations. Here, she explains why moving our bodies is crucial to our overall health and well-being.

Movement is medicine—for our bodies and our minds. Being physically active, however that looks for you, is one of the best things you can do to reduce stress and increase energy levels and creativity. When my body is in motion, ideas flow more smoothly. In particular, walking in nature has been scientifically proven to be one of the healthiest, most joy-filled things you can do because fresh air, sunlight, and plants have healing power. (Standing on the earth in bare feet literally charges your body with negative ions and electrons that detox your system.)

The simple act of moving is a reminder of how small actions can have big payoffs when it comes to health. Studies show that getting off the couch and taking a walk with a friend, for example, is good for your emotional and physical well-being because it hits the trifecta of social connection, time outdoors, and physical movement. Having a morning dance party for one—or more, if your family is game!—can jump-start a good mood. You can even move your body before you get out of bed with a series of stretches that wake up your mind and body. Cats, dogs, and babies do this instinctively with pandiculation, the full-body stretching and yawning that we do to reignite the neuromuscular system after waking up. We do less pandiculation as we get older because we jump out of bed at the blaring of an alarm, but it's an incredibly healthy way to start every day.

Exercise: Organize an Adult Field Day!

Here's a great way to move your body and have some fun. Play like a kid for a day! You can take on this exercise solo or invite a few friends over and set up games in your backyard or the park so that they can join the fun, too.

If you're hosting a solo field day, choose some of your favorite childhood activities and spend a day trying some of these fun activities. Maybe you take a half hour to hula-hoop in your house, then draw a hopscotch grid on the sidewalk and jump around.

To host an adult field day, set aside a morning or afternoon, and invite your friends and family for classic field day staples, such as a water balloon toss, tug-of-war, or potato sack races. (See the list that follows for more ideas.) You can also set up stations for games such as hopscotch, corn hole, and hula-hooping. If you want, make it a real event with your favorite music from your younger days, and include themed food and snacks.

This exercise will get your body moving, as well as create laughter and fun moments for yourself and your friends. It's a great party idea if you're looking to connect (or reconnect) with some of your tribe. Have fun!

FIELD DAY ACTIVITY CHECKLIST

- [ ] Potato sack races
- [ ] Hula-hoop
- [ ] Hopscotch
- [ ] Double Dutch
- [ ] Mini golf
- [ ] Dodgeball
- [ ] Scavenger hunt
- [ ] Water gun battles
- [ ] Egg on spoon races
- [ ] Tug of war

Exercise: Go on a Monnet Walk

I'm a member of the Henry Crown Fellowship, a two-year program run by the Aspen Institute that brings innovative, young business leaders together for a series of seminars and a leadership project to make a positive impact on the world. We would talk often about "going on a Monnet." Jean Omer Marie Gabriel Monnet was a French diplomat, entrepreneur, and financier. He never held political office, but he was heralded as a political visionary and is known as one of the "founding fathers" of the European Union. Monnet was famous for taking an hour-long walk each morning. He practiced this habit for forty years and used the time to explore ideas. When a Henry Crown Fellow went on a Monnet walk, it meant they were going on a casual jaunt to think something through.

Try this out for yourself. Go outside and walk for fifteen minutes. Take a new route around your neighborhood. Notice your surroundings, the birds chirping, the weather, the sounds you hear. Take deep breaths and enjoy the fresh air. When you return, jot down your observations and note any ideas that came to mind on your stroll. Or, if walking is challenging, try moving from one location of your home or office to another. In this case, what stands out when you see your space from another vantage point?

CHAPTER 14

Principle #9: Create Joy

When I was nineteen, I spent the summer volunteering in Honduras to fulfill a community service requirement for a scholarship. I was assigned to work in an orphanage, and it was my first time being in another country and in a different culture.

I arrived in Honduras for a five-week trip right after Hurricane Mitch, one of the deadliest storms to hit the Atlantic, had devastated the country. Between 5,600 and 7,000 people in Honduras died in that storm, and it killed a total of 11,000 people in Central America. An estimated 1.5 million Hondurans—20 percent of the population—were left homeless. Crops, livestock, and farmland—the main sources of income for most of its citizens—were decimated.

I went to Honduras thinking I was there to help after a hurricane. Instead, seeing the unity of the people during the crisis totally changed me and how I saw the world. Never would I have thought that going to a country devastated by a hurricane was how I would learn what joy really was.

Many of the people I met were not wealthy by American standards, and in addition they had lost their belongings, their community, and in some cases, their loved ones. Yet their terrible circumstances didn't affect their ability to feel joy. If it had been me, I would have thought there was nothing to be joyful about. Prior to the trip, a bad day to me looked like my phone's battery running down, my lunch order getting mixed up with someone else's, or an internet connection too slow to download a remix of the latest Mary J. Blige song. A bad day in Honduras looked like a rainstorm that had washed away the road leading to a remote village or being forced to spend the night in a small shack without electricity. Cars were upside down, houses were reduced to rubble. But the people were cooking communal meals and dancing in the streets, and the kids were walking around breaking what little food or makeshift toys they had left in half so they could share them. The locals still loved and appreciated what they had left in their lives. They made time to be with the people they loved.

Witnessing how these moments of joy sustained the many Hondurans as they grappled with such deep collective devastation taught me how joy is not just a feeling that comes and goes. By nurturing and cultivating it, it can become a constant presence in your life, no matter what your circumstances are.

Joy is a key component of the Elevation Approach and it forms the foundation of work-life harmony. Many of the earlier principles were designed to bring you small moments of joy as you work toward your goal. This ninth principle takes you beyond these instances of immediate elevation and shows you how to make joy a long-lasting presence in your life.

What Is Joy?

Joy is a state of delight and contentment. It's that deep sense of pleasure you feel to your core when you do something you love.

It has a few characteristics that set it apart from other positive feelings:

- **JOY IS LONG-LASTING:** Joy can be a prolonged, sustained feeling even after the source of your joy isn't around anymore. For example, if you're a runner, the joy of running might last well after you've completed your daily run. The satisfaction from completing your miles, the delight of the outdoors, and the fresh air can bring a contentment that lasts for hours.

- **JOY CAN BE AN INVOLUNTARY RESPONSE:** Even the feeling of a joyful thing can spark joy. Just thinking about something joyful, like traveling abroad or dinner with friends, can cause a burst of joy even when you're not on a trip or eating out with those pals.

- **JOY IS IN THE ACTION, NOT THE RESULTS:** Joy often comes from the act or process of doing something. For example, I love to tell stories. The process of brainstorming ideas for a story gives me deep satisfaction. The joy of writing comes from putting those words on a page, not whether the stories are published or not.

- **JOY CAN BE FOUND IN COMPLETING EVERYDAY TASKS:** We can experience joy when we're doing the most ordinary activities, like buying groceries, cleaning the dishes, or making the bed. I have even found joy in mundane activities like doing the laundry, and in the worst moments of my life, simply because I can do things in that moment that give me joy. With joy, you can bring more of the things into your life that feel good, no matter the circumstances.

While joy is easy to find when we're spending time on fun and meaningful activities, you can also intentionally create it. In fact, knowing how to intentionally create joy is a valuable skill that can help you get through those not so joyous times in your life. These darker moments could be small things, like when it starts raining on your morning run, or bigger life hurdles, such as a long-term illness or injury. Creating joy might mean choosing to sing in the rain while you run or running despite the rain because running in these conditions is still better than spending that time in bed.

It's possible that the things that bring us joy will change during our lives, especially as experiences expand, needs change, social circles shift, and personal selves evolve. For example, what brought us joy as children is different from what brings us joy as adults. (Many of my friends have said that in their twenties, joy was going to the hottest club or restaurant and staying out late, but in their forties, joy is being in their pajamas at 8 p.m.!)

Choose Joy over Happiness

Though we might feel both joy and happiness after doing something enjoyable, or even use both words interchangeably, they are not the same things. Whereas joy is a sustained feeling you can consciously nurture, happiness is temporary and circumstantial. Whether you experience happiness usually depends on whether you've achieved a desired outcome or other circumstance. It's often a results-based feeling. Joy is rooted in action, created when you are relishing the process of doing something.

I don't focus on happiness; that's because what makes me happy can change so easily. When we focus on happiness, we encourage ourselves to chase rewards that are temporary, that make us feel good or distract us from other things that bring long-lasting contentment.

My decision to close my company showed me the importance of prioritizing joy over circumstantial happiness. After learning that Buzz Marketing Group was operating at a loss, I went on a sabbatical and took a trip to Yellowstone National Park. I was in my element. I tracked a bear. I was walking in the middle of nowhere in the mountains, breathing the freshest air, watching the bison roam.

As I was sitting in this special place, a thought occurred to me: I didn't ever want to go back to my agency. Spending those few days at the park reminded me that this was what joy was supposed to feel like—vibrant, fulfilling, and free. I realized that being the CEO of BMG didn't give me these feelings. The agency I'd spent nearly two decades building, that had afforded me the success and platform to be on corporate boards and participate in the Henry Crown Fellowship program, was no longer bringing me joy.

I knew that trying to save my business had the potential of making me happy and would bring moments of happiness, but I knew the thrill of turning our numbers around, closing another deal, signing new clients, and launching the next successful campaign wouldn't last. Finding joy in my work would have sustained me through those long hours, the never-ending meetings, and the busy work, but I had lost that feeling after years of running the business.

When I returned home, I committed to closing the doors of BMG. Though I didn't have complete clarity on when and how I would shutter it, or what my business would look like afterward, the decision itself would lead me to more joy than I had ever thought possible. When I did shutter BMG, I immediately felt that joy. Alongside the freedom, fear, and relief, there it was—joy. I didn't know what would happen next, but the presence of joy in my life reassured me that I had made the right decision. I was on my way to doing the things I truly loved.

Is This Joy or Happiness?

Here are some key questions to ask yourself when you're assessing if an activity is bringing you joy or just making you temporarily happy:

- Do I feel content as I complete this activity? Am I smiling or laughing?
- Is this the only activity I'd like to be doing right now?
- Am I saying nice things, either about myself or my surroundings?
- Are my feelings determined by the action or the outcome of what I'm doing?
- Would I do this activity again if it didn't go as planned?
- Have I felt this way before?

If you answer yes to most of these questions, chances are you're on the path to joy!

How to Cultivate Joy

If I had the key to finding the joy in life, I would be a billionaire many times over. But alas, learning to make joy a regular feature in your life takes patience and practice. It is up to you to define and nurture joy for yourself. It's taken me a long time to incorporate joy into my life. But once I did, I was able to tap into this feeling whenever I wanted.

Recreation is the ideal phase to flex the muscles that create joy. If you're not sure where to start, here are the strategies that have helped me cultivate it for myself:

1. **NOTICE WHEN JOY IS PRESENT AND WHEN JOY IS ABSENT.** In order to create more joy in your life, you need to know what joy feels like. What does it feel like for you? Is it a tingling in your fingertips or a fluttering in the stomach? Is it a sense of calm that covers you like a warm blanket? Do you find yourself smiling involuntarily? And what does it feel like when you're not feeling joy? Do you feel stressed, overwhelmed, unfocused?

2. **TUNE IN TO PRESENT MOMENTS.** Joy should spring from what you're doing now, not from what you expect to do in the future or what will happen if you do something perfectly. Focus on what is happening in front of you. If you feel at peace sitting with a good book in a comfy chair—no matter if you've read one page or a hundred pages, or even finished the book—then reading is likely something that creates joy for you.

3. **LET GO OF RESULTS.** Do something that feels good even if you fail. As I have said, happiness is rooted in temporary conditions. Joy is a permanent, lasting result from an action. If knitting brings me joy, it can bring me joy no matter whether I finish knitting a sweater or the garment looks more like a misshapen blanket.

4. **LOOK TO THE PAST.** Were there certain hobbies or activities you loved doing as a kid that made you happy? Did you love your coloring books? Pottery? Making jewelry? Playing kickball? These activities may still bring you joy as an adult.

5. **MAKE JOY AN EVERYDAY EXPERIENCE.** Every day, I make sure I direct my time and attention to something that brings me joy. Sometimes, I have room in my schedule to organize my day around joy. When I have more free time, I make one of my favorite meals. When my day includes some housework, I fit in a joyful activity along with the chores—I'll call a friend while doing my laundry, for example. When my days are busy, I turn to my joy-inducing rituals. Making space for joy on a daily basis, even if it's for just a moment, will help you get into the habit of prioritizing it.

6. **FOCUS ON ACTIONS, NOT THINGS.** Try to find joy in things other than material items; these usually only create temporary excitement and temporary enjoyment. You might be happy because you have a nice house or a new bag, but what happens when the house is messy? What happens when the bag is a few months old? When you find joy in your actions, especially those repetitive, routine ones, that joy will become a more permanent fixture in your everyday life.

instant elevation with . . .

LAUREN MAILLIAN

Lauren Maillian is an entrepreneur, adviser, speaker, angel investor, and the CEO of digitalundivided, a nonprofit organization that supports economic growth for Latina and Black women. She has also been one of my dearest friends for decades. When I asked her about joy in her life, she shared some tips with me.

How have you created more joy in your day?
I have a series of routines I am deeply committed to and try not to deviate from, even when I am traveling. This includes having time for myself in the mornings—ideally to meditate, although that does not always happen. It is nice to have this time on my own and to be by myself.

I also try hard to make sure I have time to research and read, so I can take in information I find important and inspirational and I gain knowledge I think I should have. So much frustration, especially for working mothers and women who are trying to achieve a lot in their careers, comes from feeling as though you never get time to invest in things that are interesting to you. But routines that allow us to reinvest in ourselves are good for us. They let us show the world our greatest selves. Our ability to find joy in our daily lives reflects how we feel about ourselves.

What joy-boosting tactics or routines have you implemented?
I have always really loved taking my kids to school in the morning. That is a sacred time I never miss when I'm home. Those morning drop-offs mean the world to me and allow me to have a gut-check moment with my children to make sure they are happy. I am the kind of mom who is happy when her children are happy.

Regular exercise is also a key part of my routine. It's important for me to have mental clarity, to feel strong and good about myself. I find that the stronger I feel physically, the stronger I show up mentally. I believe when you are physically and mentally tough, you can endure all that life throws your way.

How can we find constant sources of joy in our lives?
Be open and honest with the people in your life about what makes you tick, what makes you happy, and what makes you feel supported. Avoid working based on expectations. It's hard to live a joyful life if you are living under the assumption that someone else might have for you. Or assumptions that you might have for other people. I always ask my family, especially with my children, what they need from me and why. I like having a handle on what's important to them so that I know what to prioritize and can spark joy in their lives. Sometimes, their priorities reflect mine; in those cases, we are all able to work harmoniously together to find joy. If life could only be that easy all the time!

Exercise: Journal Your Joy

This week-long exercise has you list the things that bring you joy. These entries won't just inspire gratitude; you'll also use the information you record to help you live more joyfully.

1. In a journal, write down today's date and the prompt: "Joy is . . ." Take a few moments to describe three things that have sparked joy for you. Be as specific as possible. If it's a great glass of wine, then write that down. If it's the smell of fresh sheets, great. Complete this exercise every day for one week.

2. At week's end, review what you have written. Are there any patterns in your entries? Have you noticed any trends in what does or doesn't make you feel good? For example, are many of your entries related to being outside or in nature? Do many of them involve a certain activity? Or feeling?

3. Turn to a new page. Using your observations, list the top three feelings you experienced or top three moments of joy during the week. Then, write down three ways you can make more room for joy in your week. Is there a routine you can adjust? Is there a hobby you want to make more time for or people you want to see more often?

Exercise: Pick Your Joy Theme Songs

Everything is better with music. Just as Cindy picked a theme song for when she stepped out of her safe zone, choose a theme song to help you infuse any moment with joy. That is, whenever you could use a boost, think about your theme song. Are you in the middle of a sport or workout? Maybe a Lizzo track could make that sweat session even more joyful. Prepping for a presentation? Cue Beyoncé's "Grown Woman."

Songs can also lift your spirits when you're in those not-so-amazing situations. At the airport? Flight delayed? Bags lost? What would your theme song be? Brainstorming song ideas not only will bring some humor to the situation but the exercise alone will bring a smile to your face. Any way you view it, a musical backing for your day is an instant joy creator.

PHASE FOUR

PREPARATION

INSPIRATION

transformation

TRANSFORMATION

RECREATION

CHAPTER 15

Entering Transformation

Congratulations for making it this far! By now, you might have made great progress toward your goal. Maybe you've upgraded your new daily rituals. Maybe you've found some new peers to share your ideas with and have grown your support tribe. Maybe you took a much-needed break to rest and recover. Now, you'll enter the pivotal phase of the Elevation Approach: Transformation.

Transformation is the phase where you assess what you've done and decide what your next moves will be. This is where you will take action—but taking action can mean moving forward or moving on. It's the point where you declare what you want and what you don't want to do with your time and energy.

Many people assume that Transformation is the phase where everything changes—that this is where you become an entirely different person or your plans magically come together. Not necessarily. Yes, you will be transformed, but you might find that it is your next steps, rather than yourself, that have changed.

You will learn how to determine which path is right for you.

You'll decide whether to continue with your goal and whether doing something else, something better, can be just as impactful and meaningful as staying the course. You'll also discover how to set yourself up to tackle a new goal in your life using the Elevation Approach, or to start the cycle all over again to keep yourself propelling forward. Either way, you will be at a great place, feeling content after putting your best efforts toward your goal and being confident about what the future holds for you.

It's Go Time!

We live in a results-driven world, where people put considerable weight on what we accomplish and what we produce. We fail to give any thought to what it has taken to get that thing done. This outlook incentivizes us to do something at any cost and makes it easy to believe that our happiness and self-worth hinge on our achievements.

The Transformation phase offers a different way of evaluating your success. As you might have guessed from its name, this phase is designed to act as a catalyst for change. Change might come when you achieve your goal. For example, let's assume your goal was learning to play tennis, and you now hit the court once a week to practice your serve. In this case, change comes in the form of a new routine or a fun hobby that wasn't part of your life before. Change might also come if you've decided tennis isn't for you. You find the regular practices boring, and the time you spend traveling to and from the tennis club makes it hard to spend quality time with your partner. Even if you never play tennis again, the experience has made your life different. You have learned new skills, realized repetitive exercises don't hold your interest, and know that you prefer to prioritize time with loved ones over a solo activity.

Your path to change in the Transformation phase usually comes in these forms:

- You have made meaningful progress toward your goal, and you decide to keep going.
- You have *not* made meaningful progress toward your goal, and you decide to stop—and perhaps do something else.

Both outcomes are equally valuable and will help you turn any enjoyable practices, routines, and activities that come out of the Elevation Approach into a regular part of your life.

With the Elevation Approach, success has nothing to do with whether you have achieved your goal and everything to do with having made positive changes in your life, especially changes that bring you work-life harmony. In the Transformation phase, you won't just reflect on the work you did to achieve what you have up to this point. You'll also take the time to sit with your emotions, your spirit, your true callings, and your purpose to assess if your actions have truly made your life more magical. Do you actually feel at peace with what you've done so far? Do you feel all the elements of your life are in sync as you've worked toward this goal? Accomplishing a goal, even one that is important to you, is a hollow victory if it no longer brings you joy or the process to do so makes you miserable. It's possible to reach a goal, but the work to get there may have been so agonizing you wished you hadn't begun it.

Five Signs to Keep Going

Take a moment to think about how you're doing. Ask yourself the questions that follow to determine if you should continue with your goal. If you answer yes to three or more questions, your goal is likely helping you elevate your life, and you should continue moving forward (see page 198).

1. Do you look forward to tasks to reach your goal each time you do them? Do you feel excited about the activity?

2. Do you make the time to accomplish the activities toward meeting your goal? Do you find making the time an easy thing to do?

3. Do you feel good after you do the activities for your goal? Do you smile? Do you tell other people? Do you feel satisfied when you're done?

4. Do you think about your goal even when you're not doing any work toward reaching it?

5. Do you find yourself looking everywhere for points of inspiration or references to your goal?

Five Signs That You're Done

If you're not so into your goal anymore, ask yourself these five questions. If you answer yes to three or more, consider moving on to something else (see page 200). Make space for other goals or activities that can bring you more joy.

1. Do you dread working on activities toward your goal? Do you feel disappointed, hesitant, or hopeless?

2. Do you find it difficult to make time for the activities related to your goal?

3. Do you consistently feel disappointed after working on your goal? Do you find you'd rather be doing something else? Are you distracted?

4. Do you find yourself thinking negatively about yourself or about the task you're working on?

5. Do you find yourself questioning whether it's worth it to continue toward this goal?

Exercise: Your Goal, Revisited

One great starting point for reflection is to reexamine your answers to the SMART goals worksheet on page 28. Use the following questions to compare where you were at the start and where you are now. You might be surprised to see how much has changed since you first defined your goal:

- Consider the **specificity** of your goal: Does the way you initially described your goal still resonate with you? Have any details changed since then? Do you need to amend or refine these details?

- Consider how you are **measuring** your goal: Is the way you're measuring your goal giving you the information you need? Have you been collecting data about your goal? What is it telling you?
- Consider how **achievable** your goal is now: Do the actions required to continue pursuing your goal still feel doable? Do you feel good doing this work? Are there any changes you want to make to your goal or your work to make it easier to achieve?
- Consider if the goal remains **relevant**: Will your goal still have an impact on your life? How so? How do your results so far compare with your expectations?
- Consider your **time frame** for completing your goal: Did you meet the time limit you gave yourself to meet the goal? If not, does the time frame still seem realistic? Do you need to tweak or adjust your deadline?

Keep Going!

The Transformation phase is the point at which you make a commitment. You turn something that was a lofty goal into a fully integrated part of your life. It becomes something that is easy to practice and enjoy every day.

Choosing to keep going—and watching yourself inch closer to your goal—can be a powerful experience. You've proven to yourself that you can take on a new challenge and accomplish it. The confidence boost and feeling of victory that come with that gives you a natural high. Let's be honest—it feels good to win! And that boost of confidence will embolden you to take on new challenges. It will charge your faith in yourself so that you can do hard things. And that combination of confidence and hard work means you can feel truly prepared to take on anything you want to achieve.

Now, you might have hit goals in the past. You may have hit big targets at work or won a top place on a sports team or powered through a big life event. But those things might have included some tough days—days when you felt like quitting or days when you might have lost faith. Maybe you made some serious sacrifices along the way. I'm hoping that along your journey toward your goal, using the Elevation Approach, you've felt different.

The Elevation Approach has given you the tools not only to choose the next right steps for your life but also to maintain work-life harmony while pursuing new goals. You've focused on achieving that harmony so you can work toward your goal without losing yourself in the process. Now, you should be able to do the things that make you happy outside of your work, as well as be happy while you're doing the work. I hope that by now you're proud of your hard work and are satisfied with the improvements you've made by completing the exercises and following the principles. You should not feel like you've had to sacrifice to achieve what you want. Instead, you should feel supported, both by the people around you and the strength and confidence you alone have cultivated.

I lived this very experience a few years ago myself, when I decided to take on one of the biggest jobs of my life: to become a mother.

I was almost forty, and I was ready to start a family. I didn't object to the traditional idea of a family—a husband, kids, and a house with a white picket fence. But I didn't have all those things, nor did I believe that all families had to look a certain way. Since I didn't have a partner at the time, I was happy to have a baby on my own.

I applied what is now the Elevation Approach to the process of becoming a mother. I prepared by researching doctors and fertility clinics. I gathered information, finding support and guidance at every turn. I found inspiration from the time I spent with my youngest family members, and I spoke with other women who had gone through the process of having a baby by various means, learning about their journeys. I even took some solo vacations to places I've wanted to visit, so I could feel as relaxed as possible before I began treatments. I went really deep into myself, considering whether embarking on this journey of motherhood was the best path for me.

When I returned from my trip, relaxed and clear in my mind on what I wanted to do next, I began the process. My specialist and I created a plan for me to get my body primed for having a baby and prepared for an intrauterine insemination (IUI). I felt ready and excited for the necessary tasks ahead.

Or, Decide You're Done

After some reflection, you might decide not to pursue your intended goal. Your personal circumstances might have changed, your desire to accomplish your intended goal may have waned, or you simply want to do something else. Or, you may just want to take a break and not move toward something else for some time. That's perfectly okay.

The beauty of the Elevation Approach is that it helps you feel at peace with whatever decision you make. Deciding to take a break can give you the space to reflect on your current state, so you can get aligned with what is most important to you now.

For example, I was preparing for my first IUI when—all of a sudden—Covid began spreading around the world. I canceled what would have been my last appointment before insemination. I had asked my mom to accompany me, but I was afraid we might both get sick. Two days later, in March 2020, was the first lockdown. In short, the pandemic altered my future. I couldn't go to my hospital appointments, as most private clinics had strict regulations about how and when patients could come in. I also wondered what my experience would be if I had become pregnant. At the time, many mothers had to give birth alone or were allowed to have a companion only for a few hours after the birth. The process of having a baby alone was difficult enough, but with a highly contagious illness spreading around the world, the idea now seemed even more daunting.

A few months later, I met a charismatic, handsome, amazing guy whom I ended up falling quickly for. We had an intense courtship and we knew we wanted to be together, but there was a catch: he lived in Brazil. I could either continue with the baby plan and include my new boyfriend as a part of it, or I could move to Brazil and put the baby plans on hold until I knew where our relationship was headed. With Covid ever-present, I opted to take a chance on love and move to Brazil. I paused my treatments, booked a one-way ticket, and left for the Southern Hemisphere.

The relationship ultimately didn't work out, and I subsequently moved back to the States while the pandemic was still ongoing. When I returned, I was at a crossroads: either move forward with having a baby on my own while we were still in a pandemic or put this plan on hold. Sure, the restrictions on medical procedures may have lightened as time went on, but the world had changed so drastically that bringing a baby into this new normal presented its own set of challenges.

After giving it some serious thought, I decided not to resume the treatments. Having a baby was just not the right decision for me at the time. It didn't mean children were totally out of consideration, but I accepted the possibility that they might come into my life another way.

This doesn't mean it was easy to come to terms with my decision. But using the Elevation Approach, especially the steps in the Transformation phase, empowered me to make that hard decision from a place of purpose, knowing that my decision was what my soul truly wanted or needed.

There Is No Such Thing as Failure

Failure is not an option in the Elevation Approach. Yes, it's possible for something to go wrong, and for you to fall short of your expectations, but as I have mentioned, positive change can happen even if you don't achieve your goal. It's normal to feel unhappy when something doesn't work out. But don't worry. For one, you're not alone. For two, failure can be reframed to help you feel more comfortable with your results.

Instead of seeing your outcome as a failure, consider what you have gained in the process of working toward your goal:

- **YOUR FAILURE IS ACTUALLY GROWTH.** The very act of trying something new and different requires you to stretch yourself beyond your previous limits. It exercises new muscles. It forges new connections in your brain. It requires you to learn new skills. This growth keeps you moving toward greater things and gives you the confidence to navigate them. For example, the idea of moving to Brazil during a pandemic helped me grow as a person, and the decision to come back when my relationship ended helped me realize how adaptable and resilient I could be when things didn't work out.

- **YOUR FAILURE IS ACTUALLY EDUCATION.** You have gained
  new knowledge about the world and about yourself just by
  giving yourself the opportunity to work toward your goal.
  Best of all, you can use this knowledge to recalibrate areas
  of your life that feel out of sync. For example, though my
  relationship didn't work out, I still learned a lot about what
  it's like to live in Brazil. During my time there I was exposed to the country's cultural and social norms. I learned
  about the country's housing market and even a little business law.
- **YOUR FAILURE IS ACTUALLY FREEING.** When you let go of an
  uncompleted goal, you free up your resources for the things
  you really love. For example, I may have decided not to
  have a child, but now I have more time and energy to dote
  on my niece and nephews, who never fail to make me laugh
  and teach me something new. Your efforts never go to
  waste if they help you find your way to joy.

Go with No Regrets

Regrets take up so much mental space for many people. They often
come because we might have made the safe choice or have said no
to something we wanted because the path forward wasn't clear and
the risk of failure seemed high. But sticking to the safe choice
doesn't prevent us from playing the "What If?" game (see page 75).
And when we ponder the possibilities, we might feel like we've let
ourselves down. We fall into a rabbit hole of missed opportunities,
romanticizing what could have been. *What if I had moved to that
city and started over? What if I had gone to graduate school and
made a name for myself in my field of study? Moved across the globe
for an exciting job and made a new life in a country that I've always*

wanted to return to? What if I had made time for music classes and had the chance to play at the local music festival?

During the Transformation phase, you might feel sad, surprised, or disappointed, but rarely will you get stuck in regret. Why? Because the best antidote to regret is action. With the Elevation Approach, you have the chance to make tangible progress toward something that matters to you. Whenever these questions pop up, you can say that you've created a plan, executed it, and tried your best, even if you're not thrilled with the results.

Think of me now at age forty-two. If I hadn't started the process of an IUI at thirty-nine, I might be sitting here wondering what my life would had been like if I had completed the procedure and had a three-year-old right now. I don't need to ask myself, "What if I had tried to have a baby?" because I did try—and I know exactly what happened when I did. I can spend less time putting myself through the mental misery of reviewing hypothetical situations and I can spend more time celebrating and being present in my life as it is now.

Now that I'm a bit older, I still ask myself, "Do I want to be a mom?" To answer it, I return to the Transformation phase and revisit the reasons I chose not to. Each time, I come to the same conclusion. The work I did with the Elevation Approach, especially the Transformation phase, lightened the burden that came with that choice, and still does. All the reflecting, assessing, and evaluating I did helped me navigate the unpredictable turn of events and accept the ways my life changed course. It has helped me feel content with my decisions and with where I am now.

The Power of the Pivot

If at first you don't succeed, pivot!

In business, pivoting involves trying, failing, and trying again. It involves letting go when something is not working (more on this in chapter 18), and being willing to try something else, without knowing if it will work or not. You can make a similar move if you reach an unexpected outcome or if something has gone wrong. Pivoting, and knowing when to pivot, is a powerful skill. It allows you to adapt quickly and puts you on a clear path to improving your situation.

After moving through the Transformation phase, a pivot might feel like a natural next step. Everyone has a right to change their mind about what they really want in life, even if it's as mundane as a take-out order for dinner or as important as starting a family. By the end of the Transformation phase, you should feel confident and content in making moves toward something else that will feel more fulfilling.

Back to the Beginning

By the end of the Transformation phase, you should feel content with your next steps. Perhaps you are proud of the efforts you've made to grow and embrace change. Perhaps you have come to terms with an unexpected outcome or are excited to venture in a new direction.

Transformation may be the last phase of the Elevation Approach for you, but it's not the end of your journey. As you learned in chapter 2, the Elevation Approach is a cycle. If you haven't achieved your goal and want to try something different, restart the Elevation Approach and hit the ground running. If you decide, instead, to take more time to reassess, feel free to do that. You can jump back to the cycle at any time.

If you've achieved your initial goal, you might decide to continue working on it by expanding the scope of your goal. For example, if you've successfully learned how to play tennis, perhaps your next goal is to enter a tournament. Great! From there, you can also restart the Elevation Approach (or the phase that works best for your new goal) and work through the cycle again. You can use the exercises in this book as many times as you need. Each time you do, you'll discover new lessons, collect more information, and gain greater knowledge that you can use to excel further.

As you continue working with the Elevation Approach, particularly on a long-term goal, you may find it necessary to linger at certain phases, or dip into some of the principles repeatedly the second or third time around. That's okay. In fact, it's better than okay. The more you become familiar with this approach, the deeper you can dive into the principles to fine-tune your thinking and strategize as you work toward another goal.

You can even use the Elevation Approach as a check-in from time to time to see if you need more work-life harmony, revisiting one of the principles any time you need to bring an instant lift to your life. Or, if you need to give a little boost to your everyday life, just pick the principle that would be most helpful, and enjoy!

The Elevation Approach is versatile and flexible, and as mentioned, it will become more intuitive and easier to use with time and practice, becoming second nature.

Troubleshooting: "Help, I'm Stuck!"

So, you've decided to do something, or *not* do something. You may be feeling the pressure to up the ante on something you've decided to do, or drop all activity because your goal is far off. You feel you need to transform, but what if you're not transformed? What now?

Remember, transformation is not about succeeding or failing; rather it's about assessing whether the work toward your goal so far has had a positive impact on your life. This activity is designed to help you check in with your feelings in order to determine whether or not to start the Elevation Approach again.

The following is a list of common feelings you might be experiencing after working on your goal. Check in with yourself and see how many of these apply to you. If more of the feelings from the Take a Break column apply to you, then give yourself some breathing room before diving in with another goal. If most of your responses resemble the ones in the right column, then you're ready to start another round of the Elevation Approach.

TAKE A BREAK	START ROUND 2 OF THE ELEVATION APPROACH
☐ I'm tired.	☐ I'm proud of myself.
☐ I'm burnt out.	☐ I'm eager and excited.
☐ I don't know what I want to do next.	☐ I feel hopeful.
☐ I feel like I've neglected other parts of my life.	☐ Other things in my life are also coming up roses.
☐ I'm frustrated.	☐ I've learned new things.
☐ I feel like something is "off" in my life.	☐ I know what goal I want to tackle next.

I'm Ready. Now What?

The principles in the Transformation phase will help you assess your work and gain clarity for what you want to do going forward.

The first principle asks you to **find a spiritual practice**, which allows you to connect to your core values. You can exercise this principle in a variety of ways; some people meditate, others use prayer or read sacred texts. Whatever your choice, make sure you have something in your life that allows you to see connections between you, your actions, and your spirituality.

Then, you will **make space for reflection**. This is not the time to beat yourself up about past failures or mistakes. It's the time to take a close look at your efforts, evaluate the results, and apply any lessons learned to future pursuits.

The final principle is to **let go of what no longer serves you**. After you review the progress you've made and evaluate whether you want to keep going, you'll discover that some parts of your life, such as social commitments, people, habits, and routines, are holding you back. You'll learn how to relinquish these things, even when it's hard to do so.

THREE QUESTIONS FOR TRANSFORMATION

If you've finished working through these three principles, you should be well prepared to achieve whatever goal you have in mind—or to turn your attention toward something even better. You'll know when you're ready for another iteration of the Elevation Approach if you can answer yes to these three questions:

1. Is my goal helping me live according to my core beliefs and values? If not, do I know what would?
2. Have I taken the time to reflect deeply about my actions, how they make me feel, and how I want to move forward?
3. Have I let go of the people, things, or actions that no longer help me in creating work-life harmony?

CHAPTER 16

Principle #10: Find a Spiritual Practice

I grew up in the church. My dad was a pastor. My mom's dad was a pastor, and then she became a pastor later in life, too. Every weekend, my parents would take my family to Sunday services. When I was growing up, church was the happiest place for me. I loved putting on something pretty to wear and heading to church. I loved singing the hymns with my family. I loved the music in church. I loved how everyone was full of joy.

As an adult, my spiritual practice remains an essential feature of my life. I remember reading *Conversations with God*, the book series by Neale Donald Walsch, and finding familiar his practice of asking God questions and writing down His answers. I'd been doing the same thing for years. Going to church is still an important part of my routine. I attend services regularly, and even when I'm traveling, I tune in to my pastor's online sermons.

In this chapter, I talk about developing a practice of spiritual engagement. I'm not here to tell you which religion to join or what is the right way to be a spiritual person. People's spiritual guru or higher power may vary. Many of you may not believe in a higher power at all. In fact, you can define your spiritual practice whichever way you see fit, whether it matches the parameter of one religion or borrows from several different traditions. (I use the word *God* throughout this chapter because that's the higher power I believe in. Please feel free to refer to your higher power or spiritual guide by another word, as you like.)

What matters is not what your spiritual practice looks like, but whether you have one. In the first three phases of the Elevation Approach, you've made some honest assessments of where you were and where you wanted to be. You've taken in everything the world around you has to offer and have had a chance to rest and enjoy everything you've learned. In the Transformation phase, you now check if the work you've done still aligns with your personal beliefs and values.

Spiritual engagement allows you to have a heart-to-heart with yourself. It helps you figure out if your goal will keep you feeling fulfilled; you look inside yourself and check in with your spirit. It also helps you live as your best self and stay aligned with values that elevate your life to its maximum potential. In this chapter, I break down different types of spiritual practices, explain how they can guide and ground you, and show how to incorporate more spiritual practices into your daily routine.

Spirituality Comes from Within

Spirituality is your personal set of activities and routines that create a deep connection between you and a higher power. A practice of spiritual engagement looks different for everyone, but it can involve anything that helps you align your heart with your head. It relies on both your personal belief system and a higher power that you seek guidance from. It can be exercised in many ways including, but not limited to, prayer, meditation, silent thought, and reading scriptures. My spiritual practice involves cultivating a connection to God that I always have, no matter what. My practice doesn't need to be carried out in a certain place or within certain parameters.

One of the most important features of spiritual engagement is that it happens on the inside, not on the outside. Some people connect to their spiritual practice with a person—a pastor or preacher—or a place, like a church or temple. Those means are great conduits and tools, but spiritual engagement is more than just going to church or listening to a pastor or guru and following their words to a T.

When I was twelve years old, my parents became youth pastors at a big new church, so we moved from our old church to this new church. Rather than welcoming us into the community, one family proceeded for years to make life at this new church complete hell for my parents and my siblings. They persuaded other families in the church to avoid talking to us. Their daughters made fun of my clothes, with comments like "Oh, my God, her skirt is made of plastic!" (It was vinyl, and it was very in at the time!) They spread rumors that my sisters and I were mean to their older sister, who was our babysitter. I was constantly "mean-girled." No matter what I wore, said, or did, someone said something unkind about me. Church transformed from being my happy place to being my horrible place.

Our father gave us lots of advice to get us through this difficult period. His most important lesson—and one that stuck with me for the rest of my life—was this: church is not the single or most important foundation of your spiritual practice and your connection with God. Whether people are nice or mean to you at church has nothing to do with your relationship with God. No one can ever take that relationship away, and you have everything you need within yourself to cultivate it, whatever that looks like to you. Your real spiritual practice is led by you.

That advice helped me realize that spirituality exists inside our hearts and souls. No matter what threats, changes, or challenges in my outside world, I would always have a place within my spirit to call home. How I felt in my heart trumped everything on the outside. What my dad taught me about a personal relationship with God has sustained me through many crises. My relationship to God has never failed me, no matter how tough the situation.

Establish Your Core Beliefs

Spiritual engagement helps you find harmony in your life and gives you purpose by empowering you to identify and live according to your core beliefs. Everyone has a set of fundamental values that inform their decisions and guide their actions. Many people don't realize that every single decision they make—even as mundane as what to eat for breakfast—is fueled by some core value they believe to be true!

Spiritual engagement enables you to check this internal compass and evaluate whether your actions honor your core beliefs. It gives you a chance to pause and ask, "Does the goal I'm working toward still matter to me?" When you are faced with a challenge, or even just a simple question you don't know how to answer, you can ask, "Do my core beliefs allow me to keep going? Or should I try something else?" You can also check any new opportunities or information, be it from spiritual leaders, family, or friends, against this inner voice.

These gut checks can help you feel at peace with your decisions. When I was considering whether to shutter my business, it made sense to walk away from my company on paper, but it took nine months to make the final decision. Even though I had checked my numbers, sought counsel from friends and advisers, and knew in my head what to do, I still needed to get there in my heart. I took a deep dive into prayer and meditation, and I listened to guidance from God. Once I sat down with myself and felt what my heart was telling me, I knew I was making the right decision.

Your core beliefs can, and will, be challenged from time to time, especially when something new or unexpected comes your way. They might also be challenged if you run into someone who assumes their own beliefs are the most important or only correct ones. For example, suppose a personal trainer whom you admire advises you to exercise at least four times a week, but you're the kind of person who believes health can be achieved in other ways, such as healthy eating or having downtime for rest. Or, perhaps the trainer's advice has made you rethink whether physical health should be a higher priority for you.

If your trainer's advice aligns with your core beliefs, then exercising four times a week will sit well with your body and mind, making you more likely to schedule time at the gym. But if working out four times a week goes against your core beliefs, then it won't feel good to your spirit, making it more difficult to follow through with your trainer's plan. This would be your cue to consider different paths to health and fitness. Do you believe a gentler approach to health is better? Perhaps a two-day-a-week exercise program, with more focus on a healthy diet, is a better approach for you. Whether you change the way you look at health or you disregard the trainer's advice because it conflicts with your core beliefs, the right answer is determined by you.

Core Beliefs and Your Relationships

In my relationships with others, having certain core beliefs is a non-negotiable. If you don't believe in love over fear, we will not be friends. If you don't believe in abundance over lack, I'll be moving on. I consider some beliefs to be so destructive that I don't let that toxic energy into my life. In short, being clear on your most important core beliefs can help you surround yourself with the people who share those beliefs and live by them.

Cultivate Faith

At this point in the Elevation Approach, you might have all the facts and the figures. You might even have some tangible results and have calculated the risks you've taken. But sometimes, you just need a little faith—that intangible sense your goal will come to fruition.

We all have an innate sense of faith in things we can't personally prove but feel to be true. For example, I have faith in science, even though I cannot personally prove that, say, a vaccine for a deadly virus will work. I have faith that planes won't fall out of the sky every time I board a flight, even though I'm not a pilot nor have I personally studied the physics of flight. With the Elevation Approach, faith—the trust or confidence in things we hope will work out—should underlie your activities, no matter how mundane or difficult. Even in the toughest of situations, having that hope that you will overcome challenges is what gives you the power to overcome them.

Many times, we have to make decisions without knowing what the outcome might be, and we take those leaps of faith. In those situations, the best way to land on solid ground is to think positively and believe that we're going to do so. If we don't believe what we're doing will work, it won't work. If we believe something will work, we put our heart into our actions and propel them forward to make them happen. It's also more calming to think that something will work out for the better than to think it will end in tears and despair.

Many times in my life I've taken leaps of faith, even when the decisions were complex or the chance of failure was high. I took a board position with a consumer brand even though I'd heard a few of the executives were difficult to work with. I had faith that my experience with the team would be different and that I could bring a fresh perspective. My decision to move to Brazil to live with a new boyfriend during the pandemic was fraught with uncertainty, but I did it anyway. Even when that relationship wasn't working out, I still leaned into the faith I had when I moved to Brazil; doing so allowed me to enjoy my time in a lovely beach town, meeting new friends and enjoying nature.

Call it hope. Call it positive thinking. Whatever the name, hold on to that feeling of faith as much as possible throughout everything you do. The belief that everything will work out makes it more likely you'll achieve everything you want.

Avoid Spiritual Bypassing

"Spiritual bypassing" is a term that describes how people use spiritual ideas and concepts to sidestep personal conflicts or explain away difficult feelings, instead of being honest and doing the work to improve the situation.

You may have witnessed spiritual bypassing—or been guilty of it yourself. For example, someone might place too much emphasis on spiritual power when a challenge arises, saying, "Well, God is in control. This is His will." Or they will advise you to "just pray on it," or send you "love and light." You might avoid confronting your sadness and disappointment during a challenging time by telling yourself "Everything happens for a reason."

There will be times when you need more help and guidance than usual, especially when there is more than you can manage on your own. In these circumstances, you might turn to God for guidance, or to other experts and consultants for help—doctors, lawyers, and therapists. But this is just one step. There are often many other steps you can take along the way to work through a problem.

It would be disingenuous of me to say I do not have faith in God. On the contrary, I look at examples of what people in my faith have accomplished and say, "If God did this for them, He can do it for me." It's my personal version of "If you can see it, you can be it." That said, faith for me is active. There's a phrase in the Bible I live by: "faith without works is dead." In other words, having faith is not enough to make, or explain, the real-life actions that you need to take.

Your spiritual practice can help develop faith, giving you a sense of hope and optimism, but having faith doesn't mean you don't have to navigate tough situations or confront how you feel. Faith doesn't replace responsibility or action. If you need to pass a big exam, you might ask God for guidance and strength, but you still need to study hard and complete your assignments to get the good grade. If you want to improve your finances, you can have faith that more money is coming your way, but you also have to create a financial plan that helps you save more and pay down debt.

I believe in a God who can do anything, but I also believe I have to do my part. Doing the work is equally as important as having faith. And when you pair the two, that's when the magic shows up.

Nurture Your Spiritual Practice

I want to reiterate this point: your spiritual practice is unique to you. You can choose whatever beliefs you want and read whatever texts you wish. You can start and stop your practice, set the parameters for what you believe, and choose the spiritual guides who work best for you. You should and can adapt your spiritual practice to what you need at a particular time. Whatever your chosen path, do it for yourself and not to impress anyone else. Communal expressions of spirituality are great, but owning your personal journey, making sure you show up as the best version of yourself, and learning how to be in service to others should be the goal.

It is just as important to educate yourself on beliefs other than your own and to understand why you hold your beliefs instead of those. My parents may have been pastors, but I was the girl who sat across the dinner table from my father each night, debating every biblical principle I didn't understand or like. My dad taught my five siblings and me about the importance of having a relationship with God that was not dependent on anyone else—including him. Therefore, I believe I can embrace my Christian faith while also learning many lessons for living a good life and incorporating good practices from other religions and spiritual traditions. In addition to the Bible, I read the Five Sutras of the Aquarian Age, a concept from kundalini yoga. I use inspirational card decks, essential oils, and crystals to stay connected to a higher power. I am always being guided toward what I need at the moment.

Staying in the zone of discovery with my spiritual practice has helped me become a better person and serve my community better. I have no place in my spiritual life for judgment of others, because doing so would immediately turn the mirror back on myself and my own path. I can't tell you how many pastors and teachers in my own faith have reinterpreted a scripture I thought I understood and have led me to a new perspective! My openness has given me a deeper love of my faith *and* an appreciation of those who have chosen a different path.

If you're building a spiritual practice from scratch or looking for some tips and tricks to make it your own, here are some suggestions that will allow you try a few different forms of spiritual engagement; choose the one that's right for you:

- **START YOUR MORNING WITH MEDITATION OR PRAYER:** A moment of meditation and/or prayer in the morning welcomes good energy into your day. It helps you start your day feeling grounded and at peace.
- **PERFORM AFFIRMATIONS:** Starting your day with some affirmations to set an intention for the day can be a form of spiritual practice. Affirmations can be thought of as statements of your core values; for example, "I believe that God has my back" or "I believe I can create joy with everything I do."
- **READ A FEW PAGES FROM A SOUL-ENRICHING TEXT:** Most spiritual practices have a foundational text that explains their moral values and belief system. In addition to religious texts, there are popular books from spiritual leaders that offer guidance and encouraging words that can soothe and uplift your soul.
- **SET INTENTIONS FOR YOUR DAY:** Stating how you'd like to feel or move throughout your day can be a spiritual practice. This is a great way to manifest what you want to create during the day. There is a concept in some forms of Christianity in which we speak things into existence. If you don't have that dream job now, simply saying "I will have that dream job" will make it more likely to happen. For me, setting intentions works similarly. Stating "I will have a peaceful day," "I will have a productive day," or "I will not judge myself today" will help turn these intentions into reality and sets you up for having a good day.

- **PRACTICE GRATITUDE:** Take a moment to thank God or a spiritual force for the things you're grateful for. In some traditions, thanking God for the riches you already have sends a signal that you will appreciate any future blessings that come your way.

- **JOURNAL:** Writing down your thoughts about your core beliefs, big questions about your place in the universe, and/or your moral values can be a spiritual practice in itself. Think of journaling as a way to craft a sacred text, but in your own words. Consider your daily journaling as a way to check in with your spirit and express what's in your heart.

- **ATTEND A RELIGIOUS OR SPIRITUAL GATHERING:** Whether you take part in a religious service or sign up for a meditation retreat, participating in a gathering allows you to share your spiritual practice with like-minded people, as well as find community with others who share your beliefs.

- **LEARN ABOUT OTHER RELIGIOUS AND SPIRITUAL TRADITIONS:** Learning about other traditions can enrich your spiritual practice, even if you don't choose to incorporate those traditions into your own. For example, while black is traditionally a color of mourning and worn at somber events such as funerals, my family wears white because we believe the soul has ascended to heaven and we should celebrate. This is a long-standing Black southern church tradition. It's also customary in Hindu and Buddhism to wear white as a symbol of mourning. And in some parts of the world, reds and purples are a symbol of mourning. Knowing more about these various traditions makes me appreciate my family's practices even more deeply. If spiritual engagement is new to you, learning about such practices might introduce you to one that resonates with you.

instant elevation with . . .

KATE NORTHRUP

Kate Northrup is an entrepreneur, speaker, author, and creator. She is the author of the books Do Less *and* Money: A Love Story. *She also runs The Origin Company, a group for female entrepreneurs to help busy women manage their time with more ease. Here, she talks about the importance of her spiritual practice in her life:*

I've rarely ever had a specific spiritual practice that's completely separate from my "regular" life. I am, however, an incredibly spiritual person. My spirituality is integral to my entire being—how I parent, how I partner, how I work. I infuse as many moments as I possibly can throughout my day with intentionality. It feels kind of like prayer in motion.

While I'm working out, I often set intentions for specific release or manifestation. While I'm walking in the woods, I feel my connection to the earth as an inroad to my connection with spirit. I wrap my little girls in prayer as I sing them lullabies and kiss them good night. I send prayers of love and intention to my clients as I prepare for our retreats, leave them voice messages via Voxers, or work on administrative tasks. I light a candle and pull cards as I plan my week. I set goals for my business in concert with the moon.

Living my life as a spiritual practice helps me feel safe and in trust. Knowing that I'm part of something bigger and allowing that something bigger to hold me helps me act courageously in ways that wouldn't be possible otherwise. The deeper I infuse spirituality in my daily life (through acts as simple as bringing my full presence to washing the dishes) the more connected I am with my creativity. I see myself as a conduit for what the Divine wants to bring through me to Earth, and as long as I remember this to be true, my entire life feels powerful, grounded, beautiful, and true (which is especially helpful when things don't go as I'd planned, which is often).

Exercise: Define Your Beliefs

The following questions will prompt you to think deeply about your beliefs, whether you attend religious services every week or have created your own spiritual practices. You can use them to think about your beliefs as a whole or choose one or two beliefs to analyze. Don't worry about saying the right thing or writing polished responses. The aim of this exercise is to help you define what you believe and, if needed, update or refine your beliefs.

1. What do you believe?
2. Where do those beliefs come from?
3. Where do you see these beliefs play out in your life?
4. How would you explain this belief to someone else? Or to a child?
5. What did you believe when you were a child? How have these beliefs changed?

Exercise: A Core Beliefs Alignment Guide

Now that you've defined your core beliefs in the previous exercise, check in with yourself to see if your goal aligns with them. Look at all the actions you've taken and plans you've made for reaching your goal—not just the work directly related to that goal. Don't forget about the ways you've realigned your time, priorities, health concerns, and personal obligations to make the goal happen.

Using the worksheet on page 224, write down your goal at the top of the page. Working from left to right, write down some of your core beliefs in the leftmost column. Start with the beliefs that inspired you to set the goal in the first place. What two or three core values did your goal serve?

In the second column from the left, write down your past actions. What things did you obtain or accomplish before using the Elevation Approach? Did they line up with your larger core beliefs? Did you also enjoy any hobbies that lined up with your beliefs?

Then, look at the major steps you've taken toward reaching the goal. Compare those with your list of core values to see if they are aligned. Write those down in the third column from the left.

Then consider some of your future actions. What else do you have to do to reach the goal? How will those actions relate to your core values? Write down some of those thoughts in the last column, the one on the right.

You should now have a sense of whether your actions spiritually align with your core values. This spiritual alignment will give you a sense of purpose as you continue your work with the Elevation Approach and will make your future efforts feel even more fulfilling.

Here's an example to illustrate the exercise:

Goal: I want to obtain a real estate license.

CORE BELIEFS	PAST ACTIONS	CURRENT ACTIONS	FUTURE ACTIONS
I believe in being financially independent.	Always worked for myself.	Have little debt, investment portfolio, and savings for emergencies.	Obtain real estate license to boost income and buy properties for investment purposes.
I always want to be learning new things.	Took cooking classes, learned a new language.	Signed up for a real estate course.	Take course and take test to obtain real estate license.
I believe in knowing the value of property.	Read real estate listings regularly, watch shows on real estate buying.	Completed new appraisal on home.	Take a course on appraisals so I know how to appraise homes on my own.

Goal: _____

_____

CORE BELIEFS	PAST ACTIONS	CURRENT ACTIONS	FUTURE ACTIONS

CHAPTER 17

Principle #11: Make Space for Reflection

While you may have already reflected on your goal and your progress in earlier phases of the Elevation Approach, reflection is an especially important principle of the Transformation phase.

With principle 10, finding your spiritual practice, you asked whether working toward your goal helped you live by your values. With this principle, you'll take stock of the progress you've made, putting some serious thought and consideration into your actions and their effects. This pause for reflection allows you to plot your next moves with peace of mind and will prevent you from making important decisions haphazardly.

I had to make one of these decisions when it came time to sell the house I had owned for fourteen years. It took me two years to finally make the decision, and during those two years I relied on reflection, especially when circumstances gave me compelling reasons to change my mind.

Behind my house there is a park with lush trees, a walking trail, and a field where kids played soccer. For more than a decade, there were no homes being built behind my house, and I had thought the park would prevent any new construction. The morning after I came home from a business trip, I looked out my window as I was doing the dishes and saw that half the trees behind my yard were gone. A developer had bought the land and planned to build a hundred townhouses!

Because the construction would put my peace and quiet in jeopardy, I had thought I wanted to sell. I had recently completed some renovations, so it was in prime shape for me to put it on the market. Then, enter Covid. The pandemic was the longest stretch I'd ever spent in my home without traveling or commuting to work. I had an amazing time, cooking, working, and enjoying my time in my space. I reflected on how I really felt in that house. Even with construction happening behind me, I was happy to be in the house. It was cozy, comfortable, and stocked with all the things I loved. So, I chose not to move.

A month before I decided to move to Brazil, my neighbor Steve and his wife told me they were moving. Steve was like a second dad to me. He gave me advice about when to cut down trees and when to make improvements on my house. I was devastated to hear they were leaving. How was I going to live in that house without them nearby? I reflected on what life would be like in my house without neighbor Steve. It felt sad. It felt like I should consider selling again.

As the real estate market took off, I got curious about the financial upside. After running the numbers and looking at comparable home sales, I decided selling my home would be a solid financial decision. I found a great broker and put the house on the market. But emotionally it was tough. This house held so many memories for me. It was the only home my niece, Phoebe, ever knew I lived in. It was the New Jersey family headquarters where my siblings would gather, hang out, and celebrate birthdays and life events. I felt I had a responsibility to keep it. Now, I was unsure, again. Was selling really the right move? Why was I so attached to this house? What did I want from my life in the next three to five years? Was this house the best place to create the experiences I wanted?

I had the house on the market for one day. A lovely family was one of five buyers who made an offer. I knew they were the right people because the buyer told me she wanted it to be her forever home. It was the place she wanted to make memories with her husband, children, and grandchildren. I thought about the magic they could create in this home and how this house could be their happy family gathering place, as it had been for me and my siblings. After pondering the future of my home, I finally agreed to sell after two years of reflection and reconsideration.

I never would have finally come to the decision when I did had I not processed my emotions at every juncture. Financially, the decision was obvious: I could have sold it when I initially thought about it two years prior. But after asking myself deeper questions about what the house meant to me, and waiting until my emotions aligned with my financial priorities, I sold the house when I was ready to do so. I sold when I was fully at peace with the decision.

Decisions like selling a house aren't easy, and they need our full attention, but so does buying a pair of shoes or deciding to try a new hobby, if these things are important to us. Reflection allows us to pause to assess what we really want from our actions and how best to move forward in a way that feels good and gets the results we want.

Principle 11 teaches you how to assess your results without focusing too much on potential setbacks. Here's a step-by-step process to guide your reflection so you know how to determine what's working and what's not.

What Should I Ponder?

You will dedicate some time to reflect on the moves you have made in regard to your goals. Think about your feelings as you've worked through the three earlier phases of the Elevation Approach. Think about how you've felt during each step. How did it feel when you were preparing to, for example, decide to move to another city? How did it feel to start saving money for that move? Did you make the necessary preparations to make the move? If not, why not? If not, what's left to do? And, do you still feel like moving forward?

Looking back is key to moving forward. When you devote serious thought and consideration to what you want and what you're doing, you can guide yourself to do the things you truly want. A lot could have happened between the time you set your goal and now. Circumstances could have changed; new people or elements in your environment could have come into play. Things change, and people, including you, change. That's why it's important to do a regular check on yourself to make sure where you are on your path is where you actually want to be. Through reflection, you can ask yourself the tough questions about what you're doing and how you feel, and then make any changes or tweaks in your plan accordingly.

So, what does reflection entail? While there are many ways you can contemplate your actions, it's important to reflect in a way that helps you make decisions that align with your current priorities. I've found there are four rules to staying on a path that results in elevated and harmonious reflection.

1. BE HONEST ABOUT HOW THINGS ARE GOING.

As discussed in chapter 15, Transformation is the phase during which you choose to keep going or choose to do something else. To make the right decision, you need to assess how you feel about the changes in your life. Your feelings about your new routines and habits provide important information about how—or if—this new activity is really helping to elevate your life.

Ask yourself these questions:

- How did your goal make you feel when you started the Preparation, Inspiration, and Recreation phases? How does it make you feel now?
- What tasks do you enjoy? Which ones feel tedious or make you anxious?
- What tasks do you want to continue doing? What tasks do you want to avoid?
- What feelings do these questions bring up? Why might you feel this way?
- What things or activities have you let go since embarking on your goal? How do you feel about those things no longer being a part of your life?
- What's left to do before completing your goal?

2. TAKE A STEP BACK AND GET THE BIGGER PICTURE.

Zoom out from the minutiae of your goal to see where you are heading and whether it's a place you want to be. It also gives you perspective. Does a stumbling block feel insurmountable because it's exposing a flaw in your plans, or does it feel that way because you haven't been focusing on anything else? Is your goal not the right fit for your lifestyle and values? Or are you feeling frustrated and stuck because you're not enjoying a particular phase? Say you've just started a new position at a company, and you're happy with your job because you like meeting new people and working on your assignments. But is this job taking your career in the direction you want it to go? Do you find the role fulfilling or is it taking time away from more meaningful pursuits? You can answer all these questions more effectively if you take a moment to pull back and examine your situation from a bird's-eye view.

Ask yourself these six questions about your life outside of your goal to see if you have seen an improvement in your everyday routines:

- Do you find your schedule feels more hectic since you've taken on your new activity?
- How is your relationship with yourself? Are you happy, sad, stressed, or frustrated?
- Are you still making time for other important things in your life? Is there some other aspect of your life that has suffered because of your goal?
- Have you talked to the people in your life about your new goal?
- Do you find more joy in your everyday routine?
- Has your relationship with the people around you improved or worsened since you've started working on your goal?

3. CELEBRATE THE SMALL WINS.

So often we focus too much on the final outcome we want to achieve and miss the opportunity to recognize the work we've done to get us there. Noting and commemorating small moments of success provides the fuel you need to stay motivated and maintain the momentum.

Use these questions to prompt reflection on your small victories:

- What have you learned about yourself as you worked on your goal?
- What's your biggest accomplishment so far? Why does it make you proud?
- What new skill, trick, or piece of information have you learned from working on your goal?
- What new inspiration have you gotten from working toward this goal?
- What have you fixed or improved since taking on this goal or activity?
- How much time on average did you dedicate before toward this goal? How much time are you dedicating now?

4. FIND NEW SOLUTIONS TO CHALLENGES.

Feeling stuck or facing a seemingly impossible problem when you've reached the Transformation phase can be demoralizing. Reflection can get the wheels turning again if you use the time to explore other options and dissect the issues in front of you. Most problems have a solution, but it might take some time to find it. Use reflection to brainstorm ideas for alternative outcomes.

Reflection is also an opportunity to be your own voice of encouragement. We can't rely on other people to cheer us on all the time or help us problem-solve, so it's important to know how to give yourself a pick-me-up when times get tough. Practice saying, "I'm okay. I've come this far, and I'm still moving."

Use these questions to help you work through the next few most practical and satisfying steps toward your goal:

- What skills and information do you need to keep moving forward?
- What other things should you make space for in your life?
- Is there another path you can take to accomplish your goal? Is that alternative appealing? Why (or why not)?
- If a close family member or friend were facing the same challenge as you, what advice would you give them?
- What things might you need to give up for you to keep moving forward toward your goal?
- Is there someone who has done what you've done? What do you think they would do in your situation?

The Do's and Don'ts of Effective Reflection

Before you furiously put pen to paper and start writing down your feelings, let's take a breath. The point of reflection is not only to help you assess the work you've done and how you feel about what you've done, but also to harness that knowledge and apply it to actions going forward.

As you consider these points, feel as motivated as possible to take the next right step. With that in mind, here are some guidelines for beginning your reflection:

DO RECORD YOUR REFLECTIONS: Writing down your reflections on a regular basis allows you to refer to them later or pick up where you left off. Or, use a voice recorder or your cellphone to create audio memos or messages.

DO REMAIN OPEN AND OBJECTIVE: Be as open to your feelings as possible—that is, avoiding editing yourself. It's possible to be disappointed, grateful, and anxious all at once about an event. Acknowledge all the feelings without worry or judgment.

DO USE POWERFUL, POSITIVE LANGUAGE WHEN POSSIBLE: When thinking about what you've accomplished, frame it using powerful language. Phrases like "I am," "I did," "I tackled," or "I learned" are positive ways of looking at what you've done. When you're talking about a challenge, it's fair to say, "I had trouble with this" or "I couldn't overcome this," but try to follow that with a positive observation: "I didn't make it, but I came close and this is what I need for next time."

DO WRITE DOWN ONE ACTION YOU CAN TAKE IN THE FUTURE: Once you've assessed the work you've done, it's natural to think about what you'll do next. Will you keep doing the same things you've done? You might if those things are working well for you. But what if they're not? Will you just . . . stop? Think about the one next right move you believe will make you feel fulfilled. It doesn't have to be the magic bullet that gets your goal to completion, but it can be a step where you can apply what you've learned.

DON'T JUST FOCUS ON THE NEGATIVE: Avoid dwelling on tasks you didn't do, outcomes that didn't materialize, or details that slipped your notice. Instead, look at your accomplishments. Focusing on the positive will make it easier to keep you motivated and energized. For example, you wanted to open your own graphic design business, but your target date has come and gone. Don't relive the disappointment of missing your deadline. Turn your attention to the steps you've successfully completed. Did you hire a lawyer to help you set up your business? Did you trademark the name and create a logo? Did you file your tax ID? These are all moves worth celebrating.

DON'T PLAY THE BLAME GAME: It's disappointing when we don't get what we want, but wallowing in self-blame can amplify doubt and prevent you from seeking solutions to a problem. Say you didn't get a job you were hoping to land. Don't tell yourself, "I must have made a bad impression during the interview. Besides, I wasn't qualified anyway." Ask yourself how you can improve and grow from the experience. Examine how you prepared for the interview and highlight what went well ("I brought my best stories about project management and studied up on the management training they were looking for"). Is it possible to ask the interviewer why you didn't get the role? Or are there better roles you can apply for going forward? Maybe this job wasn't the right fit . . . and that's okay.

DON'T COMPARE YOURSELF TO OTHERS: As the popular saying goes, comparison is the thief of joy. Seriously, having whatever Sally has down the road isn't going to make your life happier. The goal of reflection is to help you make your life more joyful and harmonious. No one, including Sally, knows you better than yourself, and what worked for Sally might not work for your goal.

Feed-Forward

I am a perfectionist to my core. If you're like me—type A all the way!—the prospect of receiving feedback can be paralyzing. Criticism, even if it is constructive, might bring fears of not being good enough to succeed or of feeling inadequate.

For me, I don't want to think about everything I've done wrong because I might be too scared I'd make those same mistakes again. At the same time, I want to know how to improve. I want to know every single thing I can do to work and live better—without the anxiety.

During my first year of teaching a leadership program for high school students at the Wharton School, my students exposed me to a concept called "feed-forward." It was developed by executive coach and educator Marshall Goldsmith, and it involves gathering insights about how we can approach future situations more effectively. That is, we are used to getting feedback on our work, but knowing how we could have done something better is not as useful as we think it is. After all, we can't go back in time and change how we completed a task. What we can do, however, is change what we do the next time something happens.

The most valuable benefit of a feed-forward is that it helps create an actionable plan for improvement. Rather than bracing yourself to be chided for your mistakes, you have information you can use to do better next time.

A recent feed-forward reflection period helped me realize I needed to add more support to my team. I was taking on too much, and I was not doing everything well. I had to reflect on how I was spending my time and what was the best use for it, and then strategize about how I could make better use of my time. I had to make tough calls and deep cuts, and I am happy I did.

instant elevation with . . .

TAI BEAUCHAMP

A former beauty editor, Tai Beauchamp is now a host, content creator, and founder of the beauty and wellness brand Brown Girl Jane and the wellness experiential platform Morning Mindset with Tai. Here, she describes the importance of reflection in her life.

As a Black woman who was raised and nurtured by two Black women—my grandmother and mother—I was taught that we have to make everything happen on our own. The idea of "Go, go, go!" and "Move, move, move" was what they knew. I now realize it was, quite frankly, a coping mechanism. The idea of pausing to reflect was a luxury—one they didn't often have time for, because they had so much to do, including work, college and grad school, and taking care of family members. For me, as we as women and people of color advance generationally, culturally, and socially, I see reflection not as a luxury but as an essential. For me, reflection is an opportunity not only to be present in the moment but also to learn. Reflection is not just recounting and remembering. It's an opportunity to understand what you recount and what you remember. It allows me to go deeper into who I am, who I'm called to be spiritually by God, and who I am becoming. Reflection is a time to see yourself for who you are, and reconcile who you're becoming with how you're moving and advancing toward it.

I'm in a season of my life when daily reflection is critical. I set my mindset in the morning, express gratitude for the day, and think about what the day will afford me. And at the end of the day, I reflect on what the day presented so I might be inspired and motivated to do it all over again—even if in a new way—the next day.

Reflection helps me assess what muscles I haven't exercised and those that are underdeveloped. It helps me move toward my highest self and see where I can have a greater impact. It also allows me to align my spirit and my resources with my environment. For example, I've learned in the last year that building professional relationships and sisterhood comes easy to me. Conversely, growing the type of personal romantic relationship I'd pray for requires me to show up differently. I'm keen to work on that!

If you don't think about what you have or have not been able to achieve, you don't afford yourself the opportunity to be as expansive, dynamic, and abundant as you could be. Life would be boring. Experiences would be too consistent. Too much consistency and too much comfort breed complacency. Are there any elements of yourself that haven't been deployed? Can you shine a light on parts of you that you've overlooked? My challenge to you: Take ten minutes each morning and evening to ask yourself these pointed questions. Let's reflect, grow, and build together.

Exercise: Be Your Own Pen Pal

In this exercise, you write a letter to yourself. You pretend to be sharing some updates about your goal to your best friend. Include the actions you've taken, how they've made you feel, and whether you're choosing to continue or change course.

At first, you might feel silly writing a letter to yourself, but this exercise will help you put your feelings onto paper, so you can face them head-on; it will help you avoid turning away from pressing problems or talking yourself out of finding possible solutions. Seeing your words on paper might also give you the confidence and clarity to make important decisions about your goal.

Exercise: Be Your Own Cheerleader

You've already analyzed and strategized in the previous exercise. With this exercise, you give yourself that same boost of motivation.

You will reflect on your progress with the Elevation Approach and the emotions you've experienced.

Imagine you are a football player, in the locker room during halftime at the Super Bowl. Your coach might come in to analyze the team's performance during the first half, then strategize and hype your team for the second half. Write a 30-second "locker room" talk. Celebrate your small victories and get excited for your next move.

Exercise: Conduct a Feed-Forward

Here's your chance to conduct a feed-forward for yourself. Assess your progress so far and see how you can apply what you've learned. Take a few moments to answer these questions:

- Have you accomplished what you set out to accomplish?
- How do you want to feel?
- Where are you going next?
- What things could you do to create a positive outcome toward your goal?
- What would happen if you did what you did again, this time in the future? Can you get better results?
- How could you get even better results the next time you do what you did?

CHAPTER 18

Principle #12: Let Go of What No Longer Serves You

Making space for reflection showed you what worked, what didn't work, and the lessons you can bring with you as you move forward. This principle shows you what you can leave behind.

A big part of elevating your life is letting go of the things that weigh you down. When we find ourselves out of sync with different aspects in our lives, it might be because we're holding on to something for too long. We keep an old car or a piece of furniture that has outlived its function simply because it has sentimental value. We keep in touch with certain family members, friends, and colleagues because we remember the happy times we once shared. We stay at a job or wear an ill-fitting dress because it helps us define our identity.

But sometimes the action that would bring us the most peace is to loosen our grip, especially after holding on so tightly. Deciding to close the Buzz Marketing Group after my Yellowstone trip was a turning point for me. It gave me one of my first opportunities to sit down and take a hard look at how I was spending my time. I had thought closing my business would free up my calendar, but I quickly realized that doing so still didn't give me the space in my schedule to do anything else.

At almost every moment, I was doing something that was in service to other people. At BMG, I had focused on improving my bottom line so I could support my employees. I took on my teaching job at the Wharton School because I wanted to inspire the rising high school seniors in my classes. I was on several boards because I wanted to give back to my community. I was even giving my spare time to other people, attending events or sharing guidance to people before I made time for myself. Like many women, I was giving myself to other people, often to the detriment of my own needs.

I thought about my dad, who was terminally ill at the time. He had spent more than two months in a hospital that past year, and he needed a device in his chest to help his heart pump blood. And yet he was so happy. He woke up every morning smiling, making jokes, and feeling so appreciative of the time afforded him. I asked him how he could stay so positive despite his health. He explained that he had spent his life focused on what's important. He told me, "I have my kids, I have my wife. I've had a great life and if it ends now, I'm okay." I knew if the roles were reversed, I would not have been able to say the same thing.

This is how I knew I had to make big changes—changes that were just as drastic as my decision to close my business. Over the next few months, I started letting go of anything that didn't bring me the utmost joy—or the utmost of any positive feeling. After six years, I didn't renew my teaching contract at the Wharton School. I resigned from my board positions. I pulled back from certain personal relationships, some with people whom I'd known for a while and others I felt were draining my energy.

This clearing out of old responsibilities and relationships gave way to new ones. I soon got the opportunity to write children's books again, and quickly launched several new series. Shortly after, I went into product development and was able to pivot my business back to the things that made me happy.

Letting go of these long-standing commitments and relationships was scary and sometimes painful. But letting go often leads you back to a place of peace in your life. Cutting ties to things that aren't uplifting your life makes room for the things and people that do. Even when you are unclear as to what the alternatives are, letting go of something that's not bringing harmony to your life automatically carries you closer to that place of peace. Eliminate the thing weighing you down, and you'll feel instantly elevated.

In this chapter, you learn to let go of what no longer serves you. You find out how to tell if it's time to let go, how to loosen your grip on something, and how to navigate the unknowns and the grief that come after.

Know When to Say Goodbye

It can be tough to let go of something or someone. Just as you're about to say enough, you might second-guess yourself. You might suddenly want to give something another try or somehow find room in your schedule for the activity. You might feel guilty or weak for letting the matter go.

Don't worry. It's normal to feel doubt and question whether you're doing the right thing. To help you feel more confident with your decision, try using these tips:

- **COMPARE THE IDEAL WITH REALITY:** We often place an ideal on a pedestal, even when evidence suggests otherwise. In many cases, organizing your life around the idea of what you think it should be takes you further from what makes you truly happy. For example, we want our pants to still fit and the trendy hairstyles that looked great on us in our twenties to look just as amazing when our bodies have changed in our forties. We want our aging parents to be as young and spry as they were when we were kids, despite seeing them tire more easily and taking more time with basic tasks. We want to be the type of person who keeps our social calendar full, but we enjoy quiet evenings alone much more than being the life of the party. If the gap between what you want in your life and what is feasible and enjoyable feels too wide, then it's time to reconsider whether this ideal is something worth chasing.

- **CONSIDER THE COSTS TO KEEPING SOMETHING IN YOUR LIFE**: Sometimes holding on to those old ideals costs you time, money, space, or happiness. For example, if you really want to upgrade your wardrobe, but you're holding on to pants that used to fit decades ago, those pants are just taking up space in a closet that could make room for newer items. Or, consider a membership to a club you only attend once a year. Sure, it's great when you use it, but how much is it costing you?

- **VISUALIZE YOUR LIFE AFTER LETTING GO**: Imagine how your life would change after you let go of something unwanted. If the thing you were letting go of disappeared tomorrow, how would you feel? Would you be sad? Or would you feel lighter? Would you have more money and time to spend on things that really bring you joy? If your life would change for the better, you know you're ready to let it go.

- **TRUST YOUR INSTINCTS AND YOUR KNOWLEDGE:** At this point in the Elevation Approach, many of the principles have given you valuable information. You've removed the distractions cluttering your space, explored new possibilities, and analyzed the facts and figures related to your goal. You've learned how to nourish yourself through rituals, gotten feedback from your tribe, and tracked how you're managing your time and energy. As you rested, played, and moved, you pinpointed the parts of your life that give you joy. And soon after, you carved out time to look inward and evaluated your progress. If letting something go appeals to you now, you're probably making the right decision. Remember, your choice isn't a short-sighted impulse; rather, it's the result of new insights, skills, and information.

How to Let Loose and Let Go

It's time to channel your inner Elsa from *Frozen* and start letting go. You're at the point of knowing it's the best thing for you to do. So take a deep breath and let's review your plan of attack:

1. STOP FIGHTING TO MAINTAIN THE STATUS QUO.

Forcing yourself to stay at a place you don't want to be or stick with a commitment that doesn't make sense anymore leaves you feeling tired and insecure. Instead of trying to fit yourself into a box that wasn't built for you, take a moment to regroup, then redirect the energy to defend your decision to create an exit strategy.

2. DECIDE HOW YOU'LL LET GO.

There are generally three ways to let something go:

- Reduce your time and exposure: You spend less time on and/or avoid proximity with the person or thing you're letting go. For example, you might accept fewer invitations from a friend who brings more drama than brightness into your life.
- Quit: You stop using, attending, or giving attention to the thing you're letting go. This might look like resigning from a job, bowing out of a social obligation, or choosing not to continue an activity you signed up for.
- Eliminate: You remove the offending object or person from your life. For example, you could toss out unflattering clothes, end a relationship, or stop using certain products or ingredients that irritate your skin.

3. CHOOSE YOUR PACE.

When letting go of physical objects, social commitments, or services, it's much easier to go cold turkey—if you don't renew that lease on the apartment or you opt out of that expensive app subscription service—you'll feel an instant lift. For ending a relationship with someone, it may take more time. For example, perhaps you want to spend less time with a friend who is always rude to strangers. You might start by declining a few after-work drink invitations or make dates with other friends, before ending the friendship completely.

4. PREPARE A SCRIPT OR A PEP TALK.

If you're letting go of a person or need to notify someone you're pulling back on something, you might need to have an uncomfortable conversation. Start by initiating that conversation in a calm, gentle way. Prioritize explaining your feelings instead of blaming the person. For example, say, "I feel like our friendship has been making me less joyful these days, and I think we'd both be a bit happier if we spent less time together." If you don't need to speak with anyone to let go of an object or thing, craft a short pep talk to help you embrace your decision to let it go. For example, say, "I am releasing this thing from my life because it's the best decision for me."

5. MAKE THE CHANGE.

The final step in letting go of something is . . . letting go. Release whatever it is not only from your physical possession but also from your list of worries and concerns. You've done everything to ensure that letting go is the decision that sits best in your soul.

It's Gone . . . Now What?

Now that you've let go of that thing that no longer serves you, what now? Should you have a party? Should you mourn the thing you've lost? Should you immediately take up something else? Should you replace your old toxic relationship with another?

Change is not always easy, and feelings of emptiness, regret, and fear may arise. You will work through the highs and lows of these emotions so you can be at peace with letting go—and enjoy what's to come.

Let Yourself Grieve

Loss is a natural emotion to feel after letting go. Loss includes feelings of sadness, disbelief, anger, or hopelessness that come with no longer having access to something or someone you did before. Those are big emotions to process when you lose something. And the way to acknowledge that loss is to grieve.

People associate grief with big loss—losing a parent, a loved one, or a long-standing relationship. But grief can come with the small losses, too. It can come with losing out on an opportunity you'd really hoped for. Or, it comes even when something like a pair of shoes or a piece of jewelry you've cherished is no longer in a condition to be used.

Taking the time to grieve can help you transition through those times. Grieving can involve acknowledging the feeling of loss. It can also involve reflecting on more positive times you've experienced with the thing or person you're grieving. It can include acknowledging your feelings toward what you've lost. It also is a time when you can allow yourself permission to move on.

Moving on doesn't mean forgetting what you've lost. Moving on can mean moving past the sadness and grief toward peace or acceptance. Eventually you will move on to another phase or thing that will bring you joy. Since the main goal of the Elevation Approach is to create harmony in your life, grieving can help you get closer to that harmony after you let go of what no longer serves you.

Here are some guidelines for grieving that can help you mourn what you've given up:

1. **FEEL THE FEELINGS.** Acknowledge the sadness, grief, hopelessness, or anger associated with your loss. Don't try

to cover up your feelings. Your feelings are valid, and you need to take time to process.

2. **SAY YOUR FEELINGS OUT LOUD, EITHER TO YOURSELF OR TO SOMEONE ELSE.** It can be helpful to discuss your feelings with someone else. Even sending a quick text message to a friend about how much you loved something in your life—your old car, a close relationship with a coworker, a business opportunity that you had to turn down—can be enough to release your feelings of sadness and get some support.

3. **ACKNOWLEDGE WHAT YOU'VE LOST.** Have you lost the community you built by stepping away from your time-consuming volunteering position? Have you lost out on a promotion by not taking a new assignment? Have you lost the plans you made for your family life when you chose to get a divorce? No matter how big or small, get real with what exactly you've lost. This will help you comprehend how impactful the loss is.

4. **ASK YOURSELF IF IT'S POSSIBLE TO HAVE THAT OPPORTUNITY AGAIN.** Can you volunteer at another organization that is just as welcoming and more flexible than your previous one? Can you get another promotion by taking on a project you would enjoy doing more? This may give you perspective on how permanent your loss is. Yes, there are certain losses, like divorce, that are incredibly hard and not necessarily replaceable. But for other types of setbacks, you may find that what you've lost could be reattained in other ways.

5. **ACKNOWLEDGE THE POSITIVE EXPERIENCES AND BE GRATEFUL FOR THEM.** Think about the positive experiences

you had with the thing or person, even if long ago.
Can you think of more positive feelings and thoughts to
give yourself a reprieve from the sadder feelings of grief?

6. **HOLD THAT JOY IN THE PRESENT MOMENT.** Remember the joy
that came from letting go of the thing you've lost. This joy
can help you buoy the feelings of sadness and grief.

Take Time to Celebrate

You've cleaned house and let go of something that was not bringing harmony to your life. Celebrating the things you don't do or
have anymore is sometimes just as great, and certainly better than
doing or keeping those things.

Letting go opens you up to new and perhaps greater possibilities. It makes way for new blessings. Take a moment to celebrate
the effort it took to let go:

- **WRITE A POSTCARD OR LETTER SAYING GOOD-BYE TO THE
  THING YOU'VE LET GO OF:** Writing your feelings down about
  letting go can be therapeutic.
- **CREATE A CEREMONY AROUND LETTING GO:** Create a moment of celebration around letting go of something. The
  celebration can be somber or silly—burn a candle and find
  a quiet moment of reflection to say good-bye and good riddance; do a happy dance around the room and sing "Let the
  Sunshine In!" Whatever it is, a ritual is a symbolic way to
  signal the end of something important.
- **CREATE A PHRASE TO TELL YOURSELF IT'S OVER:** The phrase
  acts as a reminder that you've done a brave thing in letting
  go. It can be something as simple as "Good riddance!" or as
  intentional as "Let better things come my way."

What's Next?

Once you've let go of what you no longer need in your life, what now? What do you do with your newfound time, space, and energy? It can be tempting to quickly fill them with something new. If you know what you want to do instead, then march forth. But don't feel pressured to move forward until you're ready.

If you're not clear about what you want to do next, take time to enjoy the new expansiveness. Relish the clarity that comes with a clean slate. Observe how you feel for a time after letting something go.

Now is also a great opportunity to dive back into the earlier chapters of this book. If you're ready to start the Elevation Approach again, this final principle sets you up to revisit the first principle in the Preparation phase: declutter your space. Depending on your situation, you could even consider your act of letting go as a form of decluttering, which starts sparking your curiosity. What do you desire, and what do you think will bring harmony to your days, now that the troublesome thing is out of the way?

No matter your answers, you have one less obstacle in your way. Whether you opt to keep going or to take a break, check in with yourself and see what feels best.

instant elevation with . . .

MARCIA K. MORAGNE-WELLS

Marcia K. Moragne-Wells is an author, ordained pastor, and, most important, my wise mother! She is the author of Heart to Heart with Women. *One of the biggest lessons I've learned from Mom is how to let go of situations that no longer serve us and how that can bring us joy. Here, she explains how that works:*

How does letting go of things free us from unhappiness?

Happiness is an emotional state that involves positive emotions and is often felt during a time of great satisfaction in life. When I am unhappy, I have found that there is an area in my life that is no longer producing positive results or contributing to my growth. At that point I take an inventory of my current situation to determine if there is something that is no longer helping me flourish or even bringing satisfaction. It takes courage, and it's not easy to let go of things we have been a part of for a long time, but it is necessary for our continued growth.

How do you know when it's time to let something go?

I ask myself these questions: What is the purpose of this in my life? How does this affect my time, talent, and treasure? Is this helping me to grow? What purpose is this serving in this season of my life? Am I doing this for my own growth or just to please someone else?

What sort of things have you let go of that brought you more joy in your life?

There have been times when I have had to let go of people. Relationships are important, but they may change during different seasons of life. I always try to surround myself with people who are a positive influence. I have had to let go of "things" big and small because they no longer served a purpose in my life. I have had to let go of jobs that seemed to be a dead end and were not helping me to advance my career. I have had to let go of memberships in organizations when it was obvious to me that my time with those groups was up. Letting go is not easy, but think of it this way: when you hit a dead end while driving, you cannot move forward. It is the same with life; when you reach a dead end, you become stagnant and stop growing.

Exercise: Make Letting Go a Ritual

No matter what you're letting go of—a project, a goal, something you no longer need—give it a proper send-off. Wish it bon voyage and thank it for the role it's played up until now. This type of ritual is popular around big transformational times like the New Year or new moons. The ritual does involve fire, so please practice it in a fire-safe environment.

YOU'LL NEED:

A candle, lighter, or flame

A piece of paper and a pen

A fire-safe bowl or pan

1. On a piece of paper, write down the thing that you're letting go of. Fold the paper in half. Hold the folded paper in your hands.
2. Close your eyes and think about that paper in your hand one last time.
3. Say to yourself, "I am letting it go. I'm setting this free. I no longer need this to find peace and harmony. I'm grateful for the lessons I've learned and grateful for the opportunity for a new beginning."
4. Hold the paper over the flame, ignite it, and drop it into the bowl. Watch as the paper burns. This marks your act of letting go.
5. Blow out the candle or flame and clean out the bowl.

Exercise: Break Up with Your Chin Up!

Breaking up is hard to do. No matter whether you're breaking up with a person or a thing or a service, there's always that pang of regret or sadness. Here, you practice how to break up while keeping a stiff upper lip, no matter how deep the relationship. This helps give you closure and you can double down on why you're letting go and moving on.

The following script gives you phrases you can use when letting go of someone or something. Fill in the blanks with whatever feels relevant. Perhaps you have a phrase you repeat to yourself to help you move on with more confidence or perhaps it's something you say out loud to someone else. (Of course, breaking up with your long-term partner or best friend might be a little more complicated, but you can use this script to help start the conversation.)

SCRIPT

I know that we've been together for awhile, but the time has come for us to go our separate ways. We've had some great moments together, but now I'm headed on a different path. I need to _____, and in order to achieve that, I need to do _____. I'm sure you have things that are top priority for you as well, so to give us the freedom and space to do what we want, let's part ways here. I appreciate what we've done together, but I'm eager to see what we do apart.

SOME FINAL THOUGHTS

Well, here we are.

You've made it all the way through the Elevation Approach. And I am so happy for you. You've taken a huge step toward recalibrating your approach to the big dreams in your life. These steps allow you to put first the things that make you feel fulfilled, and in turn, to create a work-life harmony that allows you to enjoy all the things that make your heart sing.

It's not easy to try something new. But you've stretched yourself beyond what you thought possible. You should feel that you've elevated yourself to a higher plane. You should feel that things in your life now complement one another. And most important, you should feel that you now have your road map for making your dreams a reality. And if you figure out that the reality you created doesn't fit your life or isn't something you want anymore, you can pivot.

Since I've learned to put the Elevation Approach into practice, what always seems to happen now is that I get what I need. And what I need keeps bringing me that work-life harmony. Every single day I have used some principle from the Elevation Approach to improve my life, especially when things aren't so rosy. I've revisited the principles like getting curious, or have indulged in some playtime, which helps me reset and spend more time with activities that feel good, even if they have no other purpose than to make me smile.

I've achieved a harmony in my life that may seem a bit chaotic or super busy from an outside perspective, but it delivers a deep sense of accomplishment and a feeling of great contentment. As I write this conclusion, I'm on vacation, sailing toward a tiny town in France. This is my work-life harmony in action. I'm not feeling stressed, nor do I feel pulled in multiple directions. I am delighted to have this work on my vacation.

What about you?

Remember, the Elevation Approach is not about accomplishing a set of goals (even though I asked you to think about one to get started). It's about taking the dreams that occupy a ton of space in your head, dreams that are centered on a way you think you should live, and about doing everything you can to bring those wishes to life. It's about building practices that help guide you when you're feeling stressed or getting anxious about how much needs to get done. It's about having the tools and principles you can employ at any time, whether you want to recalibrate your life to support work-life harmony or just elevate your everyday life. You can even think of it as a lifestyle.

The Elevation Approach is about moving you from a place where you feel stuck to a place where you feel free to live the harmonious life you should have. My deeply held belief is that we all have the right to elevate our lives—whatever that means. If you believe you have the right to carve out more meaningful time with your partner and children, do it. If you believe you deserve to carve out more time to be creative, find that time.

This book is not about my expert advice for you. It's about you becoming the expert on what matters most to you and on creating more of that. It's about giving you the opportunity to go through a process to gain clarity in the things that bring you harmony and to fill the precious hours of your life with more of those things.

My dream for you is that the Elevation Approach becomes so instinctive that you can't imagine going back to the way you were living before. You actually can have it all, once you decide what "it" means for you. There are choices you must make, but they're your choices. You're selecting the chords that flow together to make the sweet, harmonious song that is your life.

I believe that if you can put the Elevation Approach into practice, you will find that blissful work-life harmony that brings you joy even when times are hard. The Elevation Approach brings all the things in your life into harmony with one another. When that harmony occurs, the rhythm of your life is also in sync. Creativity will flow and ideas that you might have shunned or locked away earlier, because you felt they weren't worth pursuing, will now seem like things you can bring to reality. Remember, it takes time to see results. Life is a journey. But the journey can and should be enjoyable. I know there are many things outside our control, but we can control our reaction to those things and plan our next moves. We can transform our lives into lives that we want, one small action at a time.

And once we do it, we can use what we have learned to help others. While it may be true that hurt people hurt other people, I believe that elevated people elevate other people. I have visions of creating communities centered on readers and introducing the Elevation Approach to book clubs, meet-ups, and retreats. My deepest desire is to equip and inspire more people through my work and my life.

Thank you for trusting me with the outlook on your life. I am deeply grateful you've chosen this approach. I am committed to living this approach, and as I innovate and develop new tools, you will be the first to know.

Now that you've prioritized the things that make you happiest, what do you want to do more of? What do you want to try? This is the time to go for it. This is the time to elevate. And we're going to soar together.

BIBLIOGRAPHY

Barger, Amy, and Christina Best. "The State of Women and Caregiving."
 Caregiving.com, March 25, 2021. https://www.caregiving.com/posts
 /women-and-caregiving-2021.

"Burn-out: An 'Occupational Phenomenon.'" World Health Organization
 news release, May 28, 2019. https://www.who.int/news/item/28-05-2019
 -burn-out-an-occupational-phenomenon-international-classification-of
 -diseases.

Chudler, Eric H., ed. "Brain Plasticity: What Is It?" *Neuroscience for Kids*.
 Accessed August 8, 2022. https://faculty.washington.edu/chudler/plast
 .html.

Diener, Ed, and Martin E. P. Seligman. "Very Happy People." *Psychological
 Science* 13, no. 1 (January 2002): 81–84. https://condor.depaul.edu/hstein
 /NAMGILES.pdf.

Gopnik, Alison, Metlzoff, Andrew N., and Patricia Kuhl. *The Scientist in the
 Crib*. New York: HarperCollins, 1999.

"Hurricane Mitch." *Encyclopaedia Britannica*. Last modified October 15,
 2021. https://www.britannica.com/event/Hurricane-Mitch.

"Hurricane Mitch at a Glance/UPDATE: Hurricane Mitch." *Tampa Bay
 Times*, February 21, 1999. https://www.tampabay.com/archive/1999/02/21
 /hurricane-mitch-at-a-glance-update-hurricane-mitch/.

Mineo, Liz. "Good Genes Are Nice, but Joy Is Better." *Harvard Gazette*,
 April 11, 2017. https://news.harvard.edu/gazette/story/2017/04/over

-nearly-80-years-harvard-study-has-been-showing-how-to-live-a-healthy
-and-happy-life/.

"Mitch: The Deadliest Atlantic Hurricane Since 1780." National Climatic
Data Center, NOAA, June 12, 2012. https://web.archive.org/web
/20120717103126/http://lwf.ncdc.noaa.gov/oa/reports/mitch/mitch
.html.

Moss, Jennifer. "Burnout Is About Your Workplace, Not Your People."
Harvard Business Review, December 11, 2019. https://hbr.org/2019/12
/burnout-is-about-your-workplace-not-your-people.

"Neuroplasticity 101." *Brain Futures*. Accessed August 8, 2022. https://www
.brainfutures.org/neuroplasticity-101/.

Newman, Lucia, and Harris Whitbeck, and Reuters. "Mitch Termed Central
America's Disaster of the Century." CNN.com, November 6, 1998. http://
edition.cnn.com/WEATHER/9811/06/mitch.02/.

Oppong, Thomas. "Good Social Relationships Are the Most Consistent
Predictor of a Happy Life." *Thrive Global*, October 18, 2019. https://
thriveglobal.com/stories/relationships-happiness-well-being-life-lessons/.

Rugnetta, Michael, et al. "Neuroplasticity." *Encyclopaedia Britannica*. Last
modified September 3, 2020. https://www.britannica.com/science
/neuroplasticity.

Turner, Ashley. "The World Health Organization Officially Recognizes
Workplace 'Burnout' as an Occupational Phenomenon." CNBC broadcast,
May 28, 2019. https://www.cnbc.com/2019/05/28/who-recognizes
-workplace-burnout-as-an-occupational-phenomenon.html.

U.S. Bureau of Labor Statistics. "America Time Use Survey Summary." News
release, June 23, 2022. https://www.bls.gov/news.release/atus.nr0.htm.

Wigert, Ben. "Employee Burnout: The Biggest Myth." Gallup.com, March 13,
2020. https://www.gallup.com/workplace/288539/employee-burnout
-biggest-myth.aspx.

ACKNOWLEDGMENTS

Well, here we are. This is my nineteenth book, and I have to say it does not ever get old acknowledging the people who help me bring my work to life. A book like this really takes a village, and I am so grateful for mine.

First, to my agent, Andy McNicol, thank you for helping me shape my big idea. I've had to dig deeper than ever, but we got there. Thank you.

To my manager, Jeanne Yang, thank you for your wisdom and grace. Thank you for helping me keep it together.

To my dear editor, Elysia Liang, thank you for pushing me and taking every opportunity to make this book as good as it can be. To Marnie Cochran, Diana Baroni, and the entire team at Rodale, thank you for your support.

To Stef, I can't believe this is our tenth book. I am so lucky to partner with you. There's no one I'd rather trade voice memos with. And we will always have Paris.

Mom and Dad, I dedicated this book to you, because every

single principle was inspired by you. What a gift you've given me, to navigate this life on my own terms. Thank you for being my foundation and my safe place.

And speaking of safe places, Adrianne, Erica, Marcus, Lisa, and Will, you are my forever tribe.

Andre, how lucky I am to have your counsel and guidance. Can you believe we've done this nineteen times? To the entire Granderson Des Rochers firm, thank you for always having my back.

To my partners at Target, thank you for your support. My book is now a brand, and I am so ecstatic. It's a dream come true, and I thank you.

Finally, to every single person who reads this book, thank you. I am so honored you've spent precious moments of your life reading this book. I can't wait to see what you activate in your own life. I know it will be just right.

ABOUT THE AUTHORS

Tina Wells is the founder of RLVNT Media, a multimedia content venture that brings culture-shifting storytelling and beloved products to market through innovative partnerships. Tina has been recognized by *Fast Company*'s 100 Most Creative People in Business, *Essence*'s 40 Under 40, *Cosmopolitan*'s Fun Fearless Phenom, and more. She is the author of nineteen books, including the middle-grade novel *Honest June*; the bestselling tween fiction series Mackenzie Blue; its spinoff series, The Zee Files; and the marketing handbook *Chasing Youth Culture and Getting It Right*. In 2021, Tina was inducted into the American Advertising Federation's Hall of Achievement.

Stephanie Smith is a journalist, author, and editor whose work has appeared in the *New York Post*, *Yahoo!*, *Women's Wear Daily*, *People*, *Money*, and Condé Nast Publications. She has written twelve books to date, including the popular food memoir *300 Sandwiches: A Multilayered Love Story . . . with Recipes*, based on her viral food blog *300Sandwiches .com*. Stephanie is the cowriter of the award-winning middle-grade fiction series The Zee Files and *Honest June*. Additionally, Stephanie is a certified yoga teacher (RYT500) and creator of mindfulness games and content for young readers.